PORTRAITS OF PEACE MAKERS

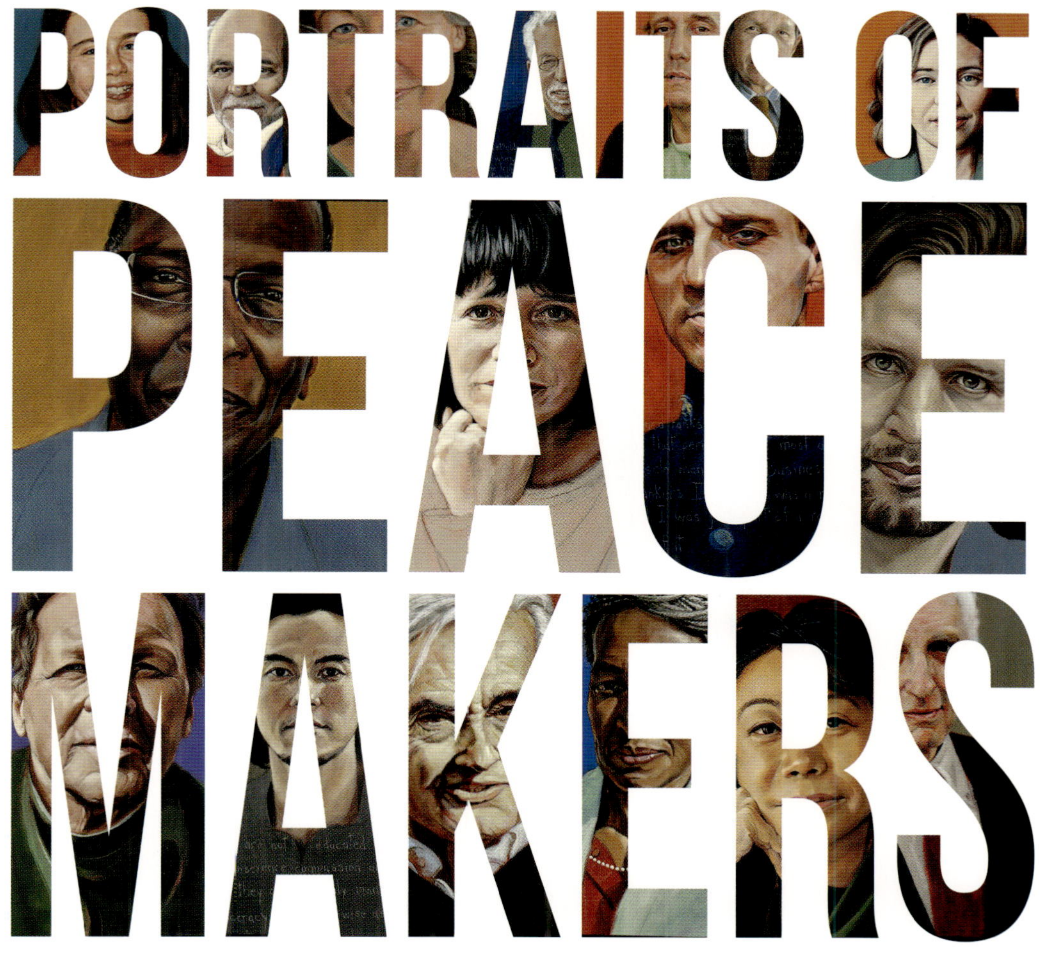

Americans Who Tell the Truth

Robert Shetterly

With essays by Medea Benjamin, Paul K. Chappell, Kali Rubaii, Alice Rothchild, Chris Hedges, and David Swanson

Aran Shetterly, Editorial Adviser

New Village Press • New York

www.americanswhotellthetruth.org
Americans Who Tell the Truth, Inc. is a 501(c)(3) nonprofit organization.

Published by New Village Press
bookorders@newvillagepress.net
www.newvillagepress.org
New Village Press, Inc. is a 501(c)(3) nonprofit organization.

Distributed by NYU Press

ISBN: 978-1-61332- 256-7
Library of Congress Control Number: 2024937885

Publication Date: October, 2024
First Edition
Printed in China

Cover and title design by Kevin Stone
Interior design by Leigh McLellan Design

Was it for this the clay grew tall?

—Wilfred Owen, "Futility"

Author's Note

I began painting the *Americans Who Tell the Truth* portraits in January 2002 as an act of defiance and love—defiance against the U.S. government's lies promoting the war against Iraq and love for the people who resisted, love for the victims. A lull in fighting when war profiteers reload is not peace. Building a culture and economy of peace is a question of survival. Without peace the world cannot—will not—solve its urgent issues of climate, environment, economic inequality, refugees, and sustainability. Peace demands cooperation, compassion, and justice. Each person portrayed in this book teaches us a particular lesson in peacemaking with their vision and creativity. They are heroes, not for going to war, but for refusing to participate. Let them be your guides.

Contents

Preface

And you must not, ever, give anyone else the responsibility for your life.
—Mary Oliver

Find out just what any people will quietly submit to and you have found out the exact measure
of injustice and wrong which will be imposed on them.
—Frederick Douglass

An earliest memory of mine is playing war on the gray rug in my bedroom in Cincinnati with small green lead soldiers—legions of them—faced off against one another. I provided the sound effects of artillery explosions and the grunts of dying men as they attacked in waves, knocking one another over.

War games absorbed many hours of my childhood—not just with toys but in the woods and streets and school playground with my friends, all of us carrying sticks as rifles and daggers. I was born in 1946, one year after the end of World War II. I don't recall my family dwelling on the war. My father was an army captain but was never sent to Europe or the Pacific. He was grateful that his poor eyesight restricted him to a stateside desk. But militarism was ubiquitous. TV and radio filled our young lives with the heroics and pathos of soldiers—cowboys and Indians, too. Idealist values—the same ones I still believe in—invigorated the power and drama of the stories. Courage, integrity, sacrifice, perseverance, solidarity, dedication to a higher cause, nobility. These thrilling values authenticated and deepened the games, giving them meaning beyond the titillation of violence. Good guys and bad guys. We learned from the beginning to dehumanize the bad guys—savages, Japs, krauts—who, because they were fiendishly evil, deserved to die, making the world safer. So immersed was I in military play that I never thought that militarism was transfused with propaganda. It never occurred to me that a primary pillar of that propaganda was that the United States didn't do propaganda; it just did what was right and necessary. Bad countries did propaganda. American militarism was altruistic.

A few years later, I was no longer playing with toy soldiers, nor running around in the woods with a wooden rifle, but I was reading war literature, some of it giving me a graphic and moral sense of war's horror—no matter the justification. My first year in college, 1965, the Vietnam War was escalating. College students were given a II-S deferment by the Selective Service, which meant that as long as we remained in good standing in school, we would not be drafted for Vietnam. The deferment was a relief, but then, as I learned more about this war—its who, why, and how—that little slip of paper that said II-S became a queasy moral burden. The government's line that U.S. war making in Vietnam was an unalloyed virtue was preposterous. The question became what to do when my country demanded I participate in an immoral war. (I had not yet entertained the thought that all wars are immoral.)

It seemed to me that if citizens were required to kill and die to save the country, my deferment was immoral. A law requiring that life-and-death hardship fall only on the poor and uneducated was outrageous. The deferment demanded my complicity by bribing me with security. And this is where the people in the portraits in this book began to intersect and shape my life. I attended an antiwar rally at Yale University in the fall of 1967. Yale's pastor, William Sloane Coffin, was inviting draft-age men with deferments to turn in their cards—send them back to their draft boards in protest and defiance. Saying, in effect, I'd rather go to jail than be part of this war. I had attended teach-ins featuring Howard Zinn, from whom I had learned about U.S. participation in the colonial subjugation of Vietnam. In 1967, Muhammad Ali refused the draft and gave courage to thousands of young men to emulate him. Phillip Berrigan and Jim Harney were breaking into draft boards and either dousing draft records with blood or taking them outside and burning them with homemade napalm.

As a result of refusing to carry a free pass from the Vietnam War, I was reclassified as I-A, which meant I would be drafted immediately. After the mandatory physical exam at the Boston army base with hundreds of other recruits, I refused to sign the loyalty oath, an act that caused me, a scared kid, to be grilled for hours by an army intelligence officer, who demanded I tell him who had put me up to this treasonous behavior. A few days later, intimidating FBI agents visited me in my college dorm room, asking the same questions. It seemed that the government couldn't believe that I and thousands of young men like me could be acting on our own moral initiative; we had to have been brainwashed by enemies of the United States.

I'm not certain why I was never prosecuted and sent to jail. I'm not complaining. But I had thought that having a lot of white middle-class kids in jail might hasten the end of the war. When they ignored me, I began teaching myself how to draw and paint.

Resisting the Vietnam War prompted me to study U.S. imperialism and militarism. Some things become clear: We will never have peace unless our schools replace the glorification of war making with strategies for peacemaking (John Hunter and Colman McCarthy); we must have history books that tell the truth about the lies told to the U.S. people to promote *all* of our recent wars, from Vietnam, the Contra War, Grenada, and Panama to Afghanistan and Iraq (Howard Zinn and David Swanson), including the failure to explain the context of brutal occupation behind Hamas's attacks on Israel (Edward Said, Rachel Corrie, Alice Rothchild); we must free our politics from the influence of the military-industrial complex (Emma Goldman and Dwight Eisenhower); war profiteering has to be illegal.

I would hope, in particular, that teachers and students would learn from the inspiring courage of soldiers who have joined the military and then refused to participate when confronted with the moral cost of what they were doing. Read about Camilo Mejía, who went to prison rather than fight any longer in Iraq. He said he was finally a free man behind bars. Read about Daniel Hale, a drone pilot, who said that "sometimes nine out of ten people killed are innocent. You have to kill part of your conscience to do your job." And read about Chelsea Manning, who understood that in a democracy the people have to know the truth of what is being done—and covered up—in their names. She was sent to prison for her truth telling.

We live in a culture entertained by violence, which lionizes its avatars. The prophets and profits of violence control and corrupt our politics. The most recent portrait in this book is that of Ben Salmon, who was imprisoned and tortured in 1918 for refusing to fight in World War I. To what horrible lengths our government went to force one man to renounce pacifism! As though refusing to kill was a disease that might infect millions of young men and render them resistant to being killers and cannon fodder. Beware the pandemic of pacifism! Ben Salmon said, "There is no such animal as a just war." Causes of war may be promoted as just, but all war is atrocity. The means make a moral mockery of the ends.

Essays of Peacemakers

Building Peace from the Ground Up: A Call to Bold Action

Medea Benjamin

A world dominated by militarism and confrontation among nations is a world that is hostile to all life-forms. Is an alternative possible? Only if we try like heck to build it.

I became an antiwar activist in high school, after my sister's boyfriend was shipped off to Vietnam in 1967. Six months later, he sent her the severed ear of the "enemy Vietcong" to wear as a necklace. I was horrified! I witnessed a polite eighteen-year-old football player transformed into a killer, who later came back home broken both physically and mentally. I learned that my government was destroying the lives of millions of people in a faraway land, Vietnam, that never harmed us. I saw how propaganda was used to demonize Vietnam and other nations labeled "Communist" in order to justify killing them. So I created an antiwar group in my high school and have continued ever since to try to build a compassionate society that does not use war to resolve conflicts.

In a humane society, we would not be allocating a staggering $895 billion a year to military spending, while so many people in this country lack basic necessities like housing and health care. In a caring society, we wouldn't lure young people into the military with promises of a free college education, but would ensure education for all, as happens in countries much less affluent than ours. In a loving society, we would not be shipping obscene quantities of weapons around the world but would be sending massive quantities of food and medicines to help those in need. In a world wracked by a climate crisis, instead of throwing money at the largest institutional polluter in the world—the Pentagon—we would be pouring money into creating clean energy and millions of green jobs.

I am constantly reminded of the profound words that Martin Luther King, Jr., spoke back in 1967, words that unfortunately still resonate today: "A nation that continues year after year to spend more money on military defense than on programs of social uplift is approaching spiritual death."

Faced with a government that refuses to prioritize social uplift, I have felt compelled to devote my life to changing the course of our grotesque foreign policy, which has spread so much death and suffering throughout the world.

My activism partner, Jodie Evans, and I started a peace group that is women-led but open to all, CODEPINK. Our mission has been to end U.S. wars and militarism, support peace and human rights initiatives, and redirect our tax dollars into health care, education, green jobs, and other life-affirming programs. CODEPINK was founded right after the 9/11 attacks in 2001, and over the years, we have protested the U.S. invasions of Iraq and Afghanistan, the arming of dictatorships such as Saudi Arabia, the gulag for prisoners in Guantánamo, the prosecution of whistle-blowers such as Julian Assange, economic sanctions that eat away at the well-being of nations such as Cuba, and the oppression of the Palestinian people.

CODEPINK's activism is characterized by nonviolent actions that challenge the status quo. Our signature color, pink, not only has served as a great branding tool but is also disarming. We have learned over the years that a bunch of men and women in hot-pink attire can lower the level of confrontation with our opponents or with the police.

We are committed to nonviolent actions, but we are certainly not well-behaved or polite. We are loud and bold and creative. We organize street protests; we camp out at the homes of warmongers; we stage die-ins at congressional offices; we bird-dog war hawks at their speaking engagements. We have disrupted presidential speeches and been arrested countless times at congressional hearings. Videos of us chasing senators down the halls of Congress abound in social media. We have purchased shares in weapons companies to be able to confront the board members, holding up photos of dead babies and asking them, "How can you feel good about profiting from a company that depends on war and mayhem and human suffering? How can you sleep at night knowing that you are, as Pope Francis has said, 'merchants of death'?"

But that's actually a minor part of our efforts. Most of the work is behind the scenes, doing research, learning about the issues, putting out books and articles to educate others, using social media to get the word out and inspire people to action.

We believe that our foreign policy has been hijacked by the military-industrial complex, which is what we call all those business interests that benefit from war—such as weapons manufacturers, military contractors, lobbyists, think tanks. It serves their interests for our nation to be involved in conflicts around the world and to continue to run over eight hundred military bases spread throughout the world. It serves their interests to keep the threat of war alive, such as a potential war with China, to justify the huge military budget.

The trillions of dollars the United States has spent in endless wars have been to the detriment of the American people. They have made us less competitive on the world stage. While the United States spends trillions on war, China spends trillions on building bridges and roads and ports throughout the world. Instead of provoking a conflict with China, we should be cooperating. Instead of fueling proxy wars against Russia, we should push diplomacy. Instead of picking sides in Middle East conflicts, we should stop arming repressive governments and, instead, play the role of mediator.

Confronting the military-industrial monster is not for the fainthearted. It is also not for those who want to see a quick fix. As I get older, I'm really excited that I get to work every day with people in their twenties and cheer them on. It's contagious to see their enthusiasm, but I warn them that to take on the military complex, they have to be in it for the long haul. They are not going to see major changes in a year or two years or maybe even a lifetime. The forces of militarism are so deeply ingrained in our society that it will take generations to overcome their grip.

That's why it's important to celebrate small victories along the way. You can work for the release of individuals or groups of political prisoners. You can raise humanitarian aid to help people in war zones. You can support legislation to cut off weapons sales to dictatorships. You can help antiwar candidates get elected; you can help get UN treaties signed, such as the treaty banning nuclear weapons. You can educate a new generation of young people about the urgent need to reverse course.

Another key ingredient to avoid burnout is to build a joyful, loving, nurturing community along the way. In this "line of work," you meet some of the best people on the planet. Try to create lasting friendships with people who hold similar views. It is the camaraderie and group spirit that will keep you going in the most difficult times.

My final call is clear: Be active, be engaged, and keep challenging yourself to go beyond your comfort zone. Surround yourself with those who share your commitment to spreading compassion and love for people and the planet. Let us, together, be architects of a new world—a world built from the ground up, where peace is not just a distant dream but a tangible reality. In the age of nuclear weapons and climate catastrophes, the future of life on this planet depends on us.

Waging Peace

Paul K. Chappell

I come from an unusual background to be working for peace. I graduated from West Point in 2002, was deployed to Iraq in 2006, and left the army in 2009 as a captain. However, my yearning to understand war and peace originated many years before I joined the military, as a result of my traumatic upbringing. My father fought in the Korean and Vietnam wars and suffered from war trauma which he brought home with him. Growing up in a violent household, I developed a lot of behavioral problems as a child. I was kicked out of elementary school for fighting, almost kicked out of middle school, and suspended in high school for fighting.

I also grew up with very strong feelings of racial alienation, because my mother is Korean, my father was Black, and I grew up in Alabama. During high school, the alienation, mistrust, and rage that resulted from my traumatic upbringing caused me to develop a mass shooter personality. Every day I fantasized about shooting the kids in my classes. My obsession with peace emerged from my childhood hunger to heal the alienation, mistrust, and rage that were causing me so much pain.

This obsession expanded while I was at West Point, when I realized that soldiers receive excellent training in waging war, but most people receive no training in waging peace. Furthermore, our society teaches us harmful habits that run counter to waging peace—habits that actively undermine our well-being, along with the well-being of others. At West Point I wondered: What would our world be like if people were as well-trained in waging peace as soldiers are in waging war? What would happen if people took waging peace as seriously as people take waging war?

I began to view waging peace as a *strategic* approach to creating positive change in our lives, communities, and the world, and for addressing the root causes of problems. Consider the problem of violent extremism. The root causes include rage, mistrust, and alienation, along with the conditions that allow rage, mistrust, and alienation to spread and flourish in our society and around the world.

I learned that one of the strategic limitations of violence is that it can only address the symptoms of problems. It cannot confront the root causes of problems or build healthy communities and societies. As Martin Luther King Jr. said, "Through violence you may murder the liar, but you cannot murder the lie, nor establish the truth." In other words, violence can kill the person who is an instrument of injustice, but violence cannot kill the lies that are capable of spreading like a virus and recruiting more and more people to serve injustice.

The lies perpetuated by extremist ideologies in the twentieth century were thought by many to have been defeated during World War II and the Cold War—political scientists in the 1990s even declared the inevitable triumph of liberal democracy and the "end of history." However, today we can see these extremist ideologies re-emerging in new ways, because in the long-term, these ideologies were stronger than both the violence and nonviolence that people were able to throw at them. Not only was violence insufficient in the twentieth century to subdue these ideologies in the long-term, but so was nonviolence, because waging peace had not yet reached its full potential—most people were not as well trained in waging peace as soldiers are in waging war.

Gandhi and Martin Luther King Jr. both saw waging peace as a method that was more effective than violence at confronting the root causes of problems, but it was a method that had not come close to reaching its potential in their lifetimes. Waging peace is a technology of ideas that people can put into action. I created Peace Literacy as a twenty-first century evolution of waging peace, as a life-saving literacy, because if we evolve this technology even further in the years ahead, we can more powerfully confront the root causes of problems, including the lies that perpetuate injustice and violence.

To create a more peaceful and just world, victories must be won on the battlefield of truth. When people think of the biggest peace issues today, they often think of war, nuclear weapons, and threats to human rights. Many years ago, I realized that these would not be humanity's biggest problems in the twenty-first century. A much larger problem would be people's inability to discern what is true from what is untrue. It is impossible to make progress on any political or social issue, including war, nuclear weapons, and threats to human rights, if people cannot discern truth from untruth.

The most common solution that I hear today for addressing the problem of untruth is, "We need to teach critical thinking in schools," but this proposed solution underestimates the nature and scale of the problem. Our critical thinking skills are only as good as our perception of reality, and non-physical needs and trauma can severely distort our perception of reality.

Peace Literacy outlines basic non-physical needs that we have, such as purpose and meaning, self-worth, belonging, expression, and explanations, among others. Trauma can get tangled in these non-physical needs, creating painful distortions that Peace Literacy describes as "tangles of trauma." These tangles include mistrust, shame, alienation, rage, meaninglessness, helplessness, cynicism, and a ruthless worldview. Digital technologies in the twenty-first century have created new ways to both manipulate and amplify these tangles of trauma.

Critical thinking is certainly important, but hungry non-physical needs, along with painful tangles of trauma, can distort our perception of reality in many ways. A person can have good critical thinking skills, but if their perception of reality is being warped by feelings of mistrust, rage, alienation, helplessness, or ruthlessness, then their critical thinking skills can mislead them within this warped perception of reality. In a similar way, a person can have good vision, but if they are in a room filled with fun-house mirrors and optical illusions that warp their perception of reality, then their vision can mislead them.

Peace Literacy offers abundant evidence from military history showing that human beings are not naturally violent. But at the same time, Peace Literacy offers abundant evidence showing that it is easy for most people to become psychologically wounded to a point where they start to descend into mistrust, shame, alienation, cynicism, rage, helplessness, or ruthlessness. When I grew up in the 1980s and 1990s, children like me who struggled with severe rage, mistrust, alienation, and other tangles of trauma were at the margins. Today we see rage, mistrust, and other tangles of trauma becoming more and more mainstream, not just in children but also in adults. When the margins of rage and mistrust move toward the middle, this threatens our democracy and the world, and makes all forms of violence more likely.

I have *realistic hope* based on evidence and experience, rather than naive hope based on wishful thinking, because I have experienced first-hand how the desperate cry of rage can be replaced with the far more powerful language of waging peace. Rage, mistrust, alienation, and other tangles of trauma can seem invincible when we don't know their many secrets, which are kept well-hidden in our society. Peace Literacy reveals their secrets, which in turn reveals their weaknesses, remedies, and more powerful and peaceful alternatives.

Humanity can no longer settle for peace as an abstract concept or sentimental wish. Together we can take peace to a much higher level, where we view peace not merely as a concept, wish, or even just a goal, but as a practical skill set and life-saving literacy.

Beware of Peace: Four Lessons for Insisting on More

Kali Rubaii

We murmur peace into the hair of loved ones as we hug them: *Salam*. Go in peace. Peace be with you. We wish peace for the dead: Peace be upon her. Rest in peace. We find comfort in the end of their unbearable pain. Peace is stitched in the hem of loss and love. But when placed against war as a declaration of politics, peace has been co-opted. Historically, antiwar movements are peppered with the language of peace but salted in the wounds of its co-optation.

The word *peace* slides from the mouths of millionaires annoyed by campaigns for fair wages—they want sound sleep uninterrupted by chants. European colonists used the word *peace* whenever people in India, Africa, or North America tried to overthrow them. It is a word uttered by politicians to justify mass killing. And it is uttered again by those same politicians to declare their wars over, even as people suffer in battle's wake.

So, I am wary of the word *peace*. In 2003, the United States invaded Iraq, killing thousands of people in the name of peacekeeping. James Mattis, one of many who designed and executed the military occupation of Iraq, told Iraqi leaders, "I come in peace. I didn't bring artillery. . . . If you fuck with me, I'll kill you all." And he did. He brought artillery. He killed thousands. Peace was a threat with an "if." And that "if" was the condition of total and utter submission to imperial violence. That kind of peace is coercive.

Lesson One: Those who benefit from coercion claim to want peace, but what they actually want is quiet. Peace and quiet: no complaints, no struggle. Nonviolent nonresistance. But as Zora Neale Hurston warns, "If you are silent about your pain, they'll kill you and say you enjoyed it."

***

He said, "If you fuck with me . . ." And we did. The vast majority of people disrupted the coerced calm Mattis was calling *peace*. Some Iraqis formed militias and fought against the U.S. military. Some Americans flew to Iraq to act as human shields against the bombs. The people of North and South America, Africa, Asia, and Europe protested in the millions against the invasion of Iraq, just as they now protest the killing of Palestinians in Gaza. Knowing about its co-option, these people rarely invoke *peace* without caveats. They say other things, like "Stop the war" and "No justice; no peace."

Such dissenters are called many things: violent, unruly, terrorists, unpatriotic, security threats. Some are arrested or assassinated. In the name of *peace*, dissenting voices are often deferred, watered down, outlawed. For example, Iraqi journalist Muntadhar al-Zaidi threw a shoe at then President Bush. "This is a farewell kiss from the Iraqi people, you dog!" he shouted. He was imprisoned and tortured, a disruptor of the peace. It was never forgotten. Two decades later, Iraqi protestors calling for sovereignty shouted, "We want our homeland." Some held up shoes as a callback to al-Zaidi's anti-imperial protest.

Lesson Two: Dissenters are always told their concerns are being raised the wrong way, at the wrong time. They are told their tactics are impolite, that if only they were quieter and calmer, they would be allowed to survive. But dissenters represent the majority, and they refuse to respect lethal decorum.

***

What are we "fucking with" when we refuse the kind of peace Mattis (who is a straw man for the ruling class and its ruling armies) offers? Coercive peace is merely structured violence that requires silent obedience from those it harms. Real peace, the kind activists call "just peace," or, simply, "justice," requires a radical disruption of resources, burdens, and decision making.

Redistribution of resources (sometimes called reparations), and of burdens (sometimes called revenge), and of decision making (sometimes called democratization) all require that structures of violence be dismantled. For example, Vicky Osterweil's *In Defense of Looting* argues that looting—a crowd of people publicly seizing goods during times of disruption—is a practice of reclaiming resources stolen through capitalist plunder. Osterweil notes that people rarely loot family businesses, but, rather, target corporate chains. This is an example of redistributing resources in the form of goods, redistributing burdens in the form of property damage, and, most important, redistributing decision making about when and how that takes place. In other words, during "peaceful" times, corporate looting does not require the consent of the people. Thus, during times of disruption, people do not require the consent of corporations to redistribute resources.

Dismantlement is a core component of building real peace. The dismantlement of coercive peace, toward justice, can be scary, especially if you are someone who benefits from the way the world is working now. And many of us, even those severely exploited, cling to coercive peace until we have a solid vision of other possibilities.

Lesson Three: If the idea of dismantlement scares you, it is time to build a vision for the world dismantlement makes possible. It is creativity time, imagination time, justice time. It is time to redistribute not only resources but also our attachments; time to let go of the coercive peace we have now, which is undeniably violent, and to embrace a world otherwise.

***

What does it mean to move toward justice in the wake of U.S. aggression upon Iraq? The U.S. never stopped bombing Iraq: the latest was in March 2023. So, stopping is step one. This might mean disrupting

the supply chain that sends weapons, soldiers, and surveillance technologies to kill, displace, dismember, and dispossess people.

Next, we have a simple math problem, or what might be called a redistribution equation. All you have to do is make a list of the things that are necessary for a society to thrive: ecological balance, healthcare and education systems, economic power, art and history, infrastructure, et cetera. Then, you add up the total of those things that were plundered from Iraq.

Finally (and this is the simplest part), give it back. The simplicity is agonizing because, of course, one cannot completely reverse irreparable plunder. But it also cracks open a vision. . . . When I run the calculation and think about where resources would be drawn to return them to Iraq, I feel the tingly rise of possibility.

Here is why: To fulfill the final step, those resources would be pulled from the coffers of the ruling class and from the bloated budgets of military, police, and prison industries, where most of the world's wealth is stored. If redistribution happened, then people living in the U.S. might also reclaim that which was plundered from them in pursuit of wars for peace.

What would it feel like to share the burdens of war more equitably? What would it feel like, really, to give back what was taken from Iraq? The tingly rise of possibility comes from the realization that it would feel like having universal health care, public education, democratic decision making, and accountability in both Iraq and the United States. A justice-oriented redistribution of resources, burdens, and decision making would be the foundation of a new world order in which the vast majority of people can reclaim so many plundered riches (of which peace is just one).

Lesson Four: It is not peace, but justice, that will build the world we want. If we let justice lead, we might find that ideas like dismantlement and redistribution have the incredible power to do more than one thing. By centering justice in our vision, we can send peace back into the murmurs of loved ones. We can demand, impolitely, much, much more. This is bigger than peace. We can have justice, too.

On Becoming a Peacemaker in a World of Trouble

Alice Rothchild

In my forties, I felt a need to grapple with the topic of Israel/Palestine, to understand the fraught issues imbued with Holocaust trauma and Israel's seductive origin story. Growing up during the Vietnam War and the birth of second-wave feminism, I needed to examine this struggle through the lens of my adult politics.

I delved into a listening tour of lefty Israelis, Palestinians, scholars, and rabbis, with a group of progressive Jews. We read the New Israeli Historians and Palestinian scholars and began traveling to the region on health and human rights delegations. In the early 1990s, the two-state solution was a radical idea, even the word *Palestine* was whispered cautiously, lest someone lose their composure along with their ability to listen and learn. Jimmy Carter had yet to utter the word *apartheid.* Once we had a grasp of the history of Jewish settlement in Palestine, the international laws flaunted in the face of occupation, and the painful personal narratives of Palestinians, we were ready to educate our communities.

I believed that if Jews really knew, their attitudes would change and the politics would follow. We understood victimization and suffering, the words *Never Again* seared into our psyches as the Good People with an intimate experience of genocide and years of sensitivity for the oppressed and downtrodden. In the United States, we marched for civil rights, women's rights, supported labor unions and immigrants. We were not in the business of hating people.

Having long given up the mantle of chosenness, I supported the work of the Bereaved Parents Circle, where Israeli Jews and Palestinians who had suffered extraordinary losses came together to find a peaceful way forward. I was moved by Combatants for Peace, Israeli soldiers and former Palestinian prisoners who joined to mutually renounce violence and hatred.

I was inspired by young Palestinians and Israeli Jews who attended the Seeds of Peace Camp in Maine and developed strong bonds as human beings, and by Israeli Jewish and Palestinian families who consciously chose to live together in the extraordinary Israeli community of Neve Shalom/Wahat al-Salam.

Dialogue and coexistence seemed to be the ticket to a peaceful future, but then the young Jewish Israelis grew up and joined the army, while their Palestinian buddies lived as second-class citizens in a country that was not designed for them, or as occupied people. The Israeli defense industry continued to find more lethal ways to kill and injure Palestinian people and to sell their "field-tested" products to repressive regimes across the world, supported by billions of dollars from the United States. Clearly, peaceful coexistence was not enough to create meaningful peace.

In 2005, Palestinian civil society called for Boycott, Divestment, and Sanction of Israel, and the liberal Jewish community fractured. It became clear to me that it was important to say out loud what so many were unwilling to speak. This was not a "conflict" between two equal, traumatized peoples. The power differential, occupier to occupied, could not be rectified through a shared bowl of chicken soup and a plate of *maqlubeh.* Palestinian leadership had its share of troubles, but it was under extreme pressure to collaborate with the Israeli military. The Palestinian "street" was becoming less willing to wait for a better day.

Listening to the voices of people who bore the brunt of this ideology, I came to understand that Zionism was born not only as a response to European anti-Semitism but from the heart of British imperialism. Zionism developed as a national movement that privileged Jews over indigenous Palestinians actually living in Historic Palestine. Zionists sought to seize, one way or another, the maximum amount of Palestinian land with the minimal amount of Palestinians. At its core, much to my heartbreak, Zionism was a racist and reactionary ideology in service of a settler colonial enterprise, at a time when colonialism was waning all over the world. I could not support that.

Israel, with political and military support from the United States, flourished as the spunky, start-up nation, absorbing a million Russian immigrants, developing modern cities, universities, cultural centers, stealing land and water from Palestinians, and creating a captive market in the Occupied Territories. The Israel/Palestine story became a tale of Jewish trauma that led to Jewish exceptionalism, violent land seizures, massacres of unarmed civilians, the destruction of homes and villages.

The oppressed people were no longer my Yiddish-speaking grandparents, but Palestinians gunned down by Israeli snipers, held unjustly in Israeli jails, surveilled by a growing web of technology, unable to get permits to build their homes, repeatedly attacked by Israeli forces and Jewish settlers in more and more brutal and egregious ways.

It became clear to me that peace without justice is meaningless, that the root causes of conflicts must be named and addressed, that struggle and co-resistance led by Palestinians is the most effective way forward. I came to appreciate Palestinian "terrorism" in the context of Palestinian "resistance." I noted that when Palestinians resist nonviolently, they are condemned with the same ferocity as when they resist with guns. At the same time, their violence is dwarfed by the Israeli military machine.

I came to understand Palestinian culture: the act of refusing to leave the land, to have and love children, write poetry and hip-hop music, embroider gorgeous dresses, *tatreez*. The tasks of getting up every morning, boiling eggs, offering olives, humus, and warm pita for breakfast, brewing bitter coffee, shepherding the kids to schools through repeated checkpoints, traveling to work without losing one's temper or dignity, celebrating Eid, lovingly caring for ancient olive groves and elderly grandparents, are the most common forms of resistance, powerful, and often joyful.

Then came Gaza 2023 and my role as "peacemaker" rocketed into "troublemaker" of the "good trouble" variety, not only condemning the war crimes by Hamas militants but also documenting and protesting the actions of the Israeli military and government in the wholesale destruction of Gaza, the killing and injuring of tens of thousands of people, two-thirds of them women and children. Resistance to Israeli attacks rapidly reached international awareness, and the call to respect international law, create an immediate cease-fire and massive humanitarian relief, return hostages, end the siege and system of apartheid, and hold Israel and the United States accountable became deafening.

As a peacemaker, I hope we are seeing a massive challenge to a system that privileges Jewish Israelis and denigrates Palestinians, that it has been made clear that oppressed people will always ultimately resist, that an overwhelming military assault only creates more wounded, desperate people with nothing left to lose. Maybe Israel has reached a painful and necessary turning point. The end of uncritical U.S. support for Israeli policies and challenges to the all-powerful Israel lobby, combined with pressure from the international community and a new generation of Palestinian activists, may bring about the changes needed for a lasting peace based not only on international law and human rights but on respect for the worth and aspirations of every individual, the end of apartheid policies, and the need for regional stability. Failing to move forward in that direction, I fear, may prove catastrophic for all of us.

The Essence of War Is Death

Chris Hedges

Those of us who have been to war carry within us death. The smell of decayed and bloated corpses. The cries of the wounded. The shrieks of children. The sound of gunfire. The deafening blasts. The fear. The stench of cordite. The humiliation that comes when you surrender to terror and beg for life. The loss of comrades and friends. And then the aftermath. The long alienation. The numbness. The nightmares. The lack of sleep. The inability to connect to all living things, even to those we love the most. The regret. The repugnant lies mouthed around us about honor and heroism and glory. The absurdity. The waste. The futility.

It is only the maimed who know war. And we are the maimed. We are the broken and the lame. We ask for forgiveness. We seek redemption. We carry on our backs this awful cross of death, for the essence of war is death, and the weight of it digs into our shoulders and eats away at our souls. We drag it through life, up hills and down hills, along the roads, into the most intimate recesses of our lives. It never leaves us. Those who know us best know that there is something unspeakable and evil many of us harbor within us. This evil is intimate. It is personal. We do not speak its name. It is the evil of things done and things left undone. It is the evil of war.

We do not speak of war. War is captured only in the long, vacant stares, in the silences, in the trembling fingers, in the memories most of us keep buried deep within us, in the tears.

It is impossible to portray war. Narratives, even antiwar narratives, make the irrational rational. They make the incomprehensible comprehensible. They make the illogical logical. They make the despicable beautiful. All words and images, all discussions, all films, all evocations of war, good or bad, are an obscenity. There is nothing to say. There are only the scars and wounds. These we carry within us. These we cannot articulate. The horror. The horror.

War gives to its killers a God-like power to revoke another person's charter to live on this Earth. Those who have felt and exercised that power have turned human beings into objects. And in that process of killing, they, too, became objects, machines, instruments of death, war's victimizers and war's victims. And they do not want to be machines again.

We wander through life with the deadness of war within us. There is no escape. There is no peace. We know an awful truth, an existential truth. War exposed the lies of patriotism and collective virtue of the nation that our churches, our schools, our press, our movies, our books, our government told us about ourselves, about who we were. And we see through these illusions. But those who speak this truth are cast out. Ghosts. Strangers in a strange land.

Who are our brothers and sisters? Who is our family? Whom have we become? We have become those whom we once despised. We have become the enemy. Our mother is the mother grieving over her murdered child, and we murdered this child, in a mud-walled village of Afghanistan or a sand-filled cemetery in Fallujah. Our father is the father lying on a pallet in a hut, paralyzed by the blast from an iron fragmentation bomb. Our sister lives in poverty in a refugee camp outside Kabul, widowed, desperately poor, raising her children alone. Our brother, yes, our brother, is in the Taliban, the Iraqi insurgency, al-Qaeda and Hamas. And he has an automatic rifle. And he kills. And he is becoming us. War is always the same plague. It imparts the same deadly virus. It teaches us to deny another's humanity, worth, being, and to kill and be killed.

There are days we wish we were whole. We wish we could put down this cross. We envy those who, in their innocence, believe in the innate goodness of America and the righteousness of war and celebrate what we know is despicable. And sometimes it makes us wish for death, for the peace of it. But we know, too, the awful truth, as James Baldwin wrote, that "people who shut their eyes to reality simply invite their own destruction, and anyone who insists on remaining in a state of innocence long after that innocence is dead turns himself into a monster." And we would rather be maimed and broken and in pain than be a monster, and some of us, once, were monsters.

Trauma is not static. It is dynamic. It is written on our flesh. These scars keep us honest if we use them to see our face in the enemy. If truth is to be heard, as Theodor Adorno wrote, suffering must be allowed to speak.

Flannery O'Connor recognized that the moral life always entails confrontation with the world. She wrote, "St. Cyril of Jerusalem, in instructing catechumens, wrote: 'The dragon sits by the side of the road, watching those who pass. Beware lest he devour you. We go to the Father of Souls, but it is necessary to pass by the dragon.' No matter what form the dragon may take, it is of this mysterious passage past him, or into his jaws, that stories of any depth will always be concerned to tell, and this being the case, it requires considerable courage at any time, in any country, not to turn away from the storyteller."

We can never be healed. Our wounds, visible and invisible, are permanent. It will not be better. We cannot impart to you the cheerful and childish optimism that is the curse of America. We can only tell you to stand up, to pick up your cross, to keep moving. We can only tell you that you must always defy the forces that eat away at you, at the nation—this plague of war.

"Sometimes I feel like a motherless child / A long ways from home / A long ways from home . . ."

War is a business. Across our country lies a labyrinth of military industries that produce nothing but machines of death. It is death we defy, not our own death, but the vast enterprise of death. The dark, primeval lusts for power and personal wealth, the hypermasculine language of war and patriotism, used to justify the slaughter of the weak and the innocent and mock justice. We will not use these words of war.

We cannot flee from evil. Some of us have tried through drink and drugs and self-destructiveness. Evil is always with us. It is because we know evil, our own evil, that we do not let go, do not surrender. It is because we know evil that we resist. It is because we know violence that we are nonviolent. And we know that it is not about us; war taught us that. It is about the other, lying by the side of the road. It is about reaching down in defiance of creeds and oaths, in defiance of religion and nationality, and lifting our enemy up. All acts of healing and love—and the defiance of war is an affirmation of love—allow us to shout out to the vast powers of the universe that, however broken we are, we are not helpless, however much we despair, we are not without hope, however weak we may feel, we will always, always, always resist. And it is in this act of resistance that we find salvation.

Why Sign a Declaration of Peace

David Swanson

At World BEYOND War and other groups that I work for and work with, we often flood elected officials with emails or phone calls—or bodies in their offices—with very urgent and specific demands to stop killing particular populations. At the same time, at the height of crises and otherwise, we find it valuable to press in a different direction. We don't want one nation saved and some other nation bombed. We don't want the weapons of mass murder sent to a different military, one that won't use them right now but later, or one that won't use them on exactly the same people we're concerned about today but on some other people on another day. We don't want the new base built in someone else's fields instead of those we are defending in this moment. We want the entire enterprise of war left behind. We want all that energy and money invested in urgent human and environmental needs rather than in mass slaughter, destruction, and the risking of an apocalyptic World War III.

Of course, in some parts of the world, many people don't agree with that. We have created countless reading, listening, and viewing materials and courses to help people reach that understanding. But for those who do agree with abolishing war, the Declaration of Peace, or Peace Pledge (found online at https://worldbeyondwar.org) is how we demonstrate our numbers, our reach, our determination, and our vision to institutions that have a hard time thinking past next week.

We're building on a rich history. On October 16, 1934, the Peace Pledge Union, the oldest secular pacifist organization in Great Britain, was begun. Its creation was sparked by a letter in *The Manchester Guardian* written by a well-known pacifist named Dick Sheppard. The letter invited all men of so-called fighting age to send Sheppard a postcard stating

their commitment to "renounce war and never again to support another." Within two days, 2,500 men responded, and, over the next few months, a new antiwar organization with 100,000 members took shape. It became known as "the Peace Pledge Union" because all of its members took the following pledge: "War is a crime against humanity. I renounce war and am therefore determined not to support any kind of war. I am also determined to work for the removal of all causes of war."

On April 12, 1935, some 175,000 college students across the United States engaged in classroom strikes and peaceful demonstrations in which they pledged never to participate in an armed conflict. Student antiwar mobilizations in the United States grew from 25,000 in 1934 to 500,000 in 1936, each held in April to mark the month the United States had entered World War I. These young people pledged to oppose all war. They advanced our understanding of peace, supported unprecedented accountability for war profiteers, and seeded the non-violent movements that would grow from the war-resister prisons of World War II into the civil rights and peace movements of the 1950s and 1960s.

Of course, war has never stopped. And the single most mythologized war of Western culture was waged in the 1940s. But opposition to war has steadily progressed.

Ten years ago, we created World BEYOND War, and we created a new Declaration of Peace. It reads:

I understand that wars and militarism make us less safe rather than protect us, that they kill, injure and traumatize adults, children and infants, severely damage the natural environment, erode civil liberties, and drain our economies, siphoning resources from life-affirming activities. I commit to engage in and support nonviolent efforts to end all war and preparations for war and to create a sustainable and just peace.

What does that mean, exactly?

- Wars and militarism: By wars, we mean the organized, armed, mass use of deadly violence; and by militarism, we mean preparations for war, including the building of weapons and militaries and the creation of cultures supportive of war. We reject the *myths* that usually support war and militarism.
- Less safe: We are *endangered by* wars, weapons testing, other impacts of militarism, and the risking of nuclear apocalypse.
- Kill, injure, and traumatize: War is a *leading cause* of death and suffering.
- Damage the environment: War and militarism are *major destroyers* of climate, land, and water.
- Erode civil liberties: War is the *central justification* for government secrecy and the erosion of rights.
- Drain economies: War impoverishes us.
- Siphoning resources: War wastes *two trillion dollars* a year that could do a world of good. This is the primary way in which war kills.
- Nonviolent efforts: These include *everything* from educational events to art to lobbying to divestment to protesting to standing in front of trucks full of weapons.

- Sustainable and just peace: Nonviolent activism not only succeeds more than war at the things war is supposedly for—ending occupations and invasions and tyranny. It also is more likely to result in a long-lasting peace, a peace that is stable because not accompanied by injustice, bitterness, and thirst for revenge, a peace based on respect for the rights of all.

The Declaration of Peace, or Peace Pledge, has been signed by over nine hundred organizations and by individuals (many well known) in 197 nations since we began it in 2014. It can be signed by individuals and organizations online or on paper.

We believe it has the potential to do vastly more, if every concerned person sets aside his or her learned helplessness, corporate-created powerlessness, and self-indulgent despair (we all have some of it), and invests much less time than it has taken to read this far in this essay to *sign the pledge.*

One way the pledge helps us build a movement to end all wars is through numbers. Another is through alliances with organizations across the full spectrum of human activities.

Opposition to war has been bizarrely omitted from most cross-issue coalitions and movements. Reinstalling peace as a part of progressive values could unlock vast potential for many movements that can be stronger together.

The Portraits

Jane Addams

Social reformer; b. 1860, d. 1935

. . . much of the insensibility and hardness of the world is due to the lack of imagination which prevents a realization of the experience of other people.

If one were to put a face to the social activism of the Progressive Era (1890–1920), Laura Jane Addams would be the natural choice. Not only a trailblazer in the fields of social work and sociology, she was also a leader of the peace movement and the struggle for women's suffrage.

Addams was born on September 6, 1860, in Cedarville, Illinois, to John and Sarah Addams, their eighth child of nine. John Addams, a former Illinois state senator, was one of the founders of the Illinois Republican Party. Addams graduated from the Rockford Female Seminary in 1881 and then attended medical school at the Woman's Medical College of Philadelphia. But because of multiple health issues, she was unable to complete her medical education.

During a trip to England, Addams visited Toynbee Hall, a settlement house for the poor, established by Samuel and Henrietta Barnett in 1884. Following the Barnetts' model and with the help of her close friend Ellen Gates Starr, Addams founded Hull House in Chicago. Opened in 1886, it was one of the first settlement house in the United States.

The original mission of Hull House was to offer educational programs for newly arrived immigrants. Then Addams and Starr recognized the need to provide more comprehensive social and cultural services to their residents, as well as to the broader neighborhood. As Hull House grew, it provided kindergarten and evening classes, a public kitchen and library, an art gallery, a gymnasium, and a training facility for social workers among its many services.

Hull House became an incubator of progressive ideas—women's ideas. The volunteers at Hull House created the Immigrants' Protective League and the nation's first juvenile court. They also worked to increase protections for women and children in the workplace, achieving the passage of legislation regulating child labor in 1916. Seeing how implementation of their progressive policies was impossible without the backing of men, Addams joined the effort to win the women's right to vote.

Addams wrote and lectured extensively, and she penned two autobiographies, *Twenty Years at Hull-House* (1910) and *The Second Twenty Years at Hull-House* (1930). Although Addams turned down the offer of a position at the University of Chicago, the school's sociology department adopted Hull House's documentation methods. Addams was the first female president of the National Conference of Charities and Corrections and was a strong supporter of both the National Association for the Advancement of Colored People (NAACP) and the American Civil Liberties Union (ACLU).

At the turn of the twentieth century, following the Spanish-American War, Addams joined the peace movement. Following a series of lectures she presented at the University of Wisconsin, Addams published the book *Newer Ideals of Peace* (1907). She was named chair of the Women's Peace Party, president of the International Congress of Women (ICW), and president of the Women's International League for Peace and Freedom (WILPF). When Addams severely criticized the United States' entrance into World War I, she was denounced by many. Her activism in the peace movement earned her the Nobel Peace Prize in 1931; she was the first American woman to receive the award.

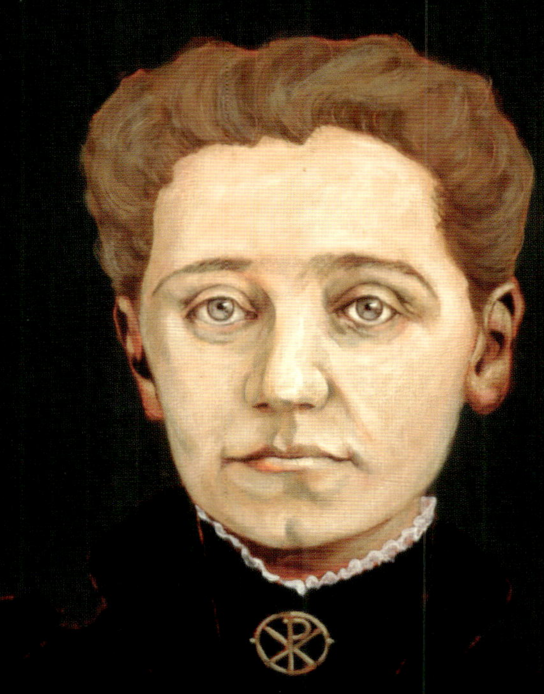
. . . much of the insensibility and hardness
of the world is due to the lack of imagination
which prevents a realization of the
experience of other people.

Jane Addams

Stacy Bannerman

Activist; b. 1965

If we have a spiritual, moral, and humanitarian mandate to alleviate suffering,
then surely we are ordained not to inflict it.

Born and raised in North Dakota, Stacy Bannerman became an activist in the third grade when she drafted a Bill of Rights for the Will-Moore Elementary School. The document was handwritten in large, carefully drawn block letters and signed in crayon by her classmates. It demanded equitable bathroom breaks, longer recesses, and after-school sports for girls. Stacy also led a sit-in in the girls' bathroom and wrestled on the boys' team.

After earning degrees in women's studies and international relations, Bannerman served as the first white executive director of the Martin Luther King Jr. Outreach Center in Spokane, Washington. Then, soon after Bannerman and her husband moved to the Seattle area, he was mobilized with the Army National Guard to go to war in Iraq, a war she had protested since before it had begun. Bannerman joined Military Families Speak Out, calling for an end to the war. She learned to navigate the tightrope of advocating for post-9/11 veterans and their families while also actively opposing the war, earning the respect of both the peace movement and the Pentagon. She testified before Congress multiple times; wrote dozens of articles, and published her first book, *When the War Came Home: The Inside Story of Reservists and the Families They Leave Behind* (2006).

Bennerman's relentless determination led to the first congressional hearing on the impacts of war on families of veterans. She wrote and secured passage of an Oregon bill that required employers to grant up to two weeks of unpaid leave for immediate family members before, during, or after a loved one's deployment. Another bill created Oregon's Military Family Task Force. Then she successfully initiated

and advocated for the Supporting Military Families Act of 2009.

Tragically, Bannerman's veteran husband, suffering from combat-related trauma, became violent and, in one of many nightmarish episodes, strangled her to the point of unconsciousness. Her experiences as a victim of domestic abuse motivated her to speak out about the frequency and severity of combat veteran violence and to engage in policy work with the Oregon Department of Justice. Her husband began using crystal meth to self-medicate, ultimately forcing Bannerman to flee. She lost everything: her income, her health care, her home, her animals; then another crystal meth user stole her identity. She wrote about her experiences in her second book, *Homefront 911: How Families of Veterans Are Wounded by Our Wars* (2015).

After emerging from these personal traumas, Bannerman made the connection between warfare and climate collapse, and this became a new focus of her work. She founded Women's EcoPeace and launched a national Divest from War campaign in the summer of 2018. She also led the Heart2Heart Tour to Philadelphia's Constitution Center, where she gave her Freedom Medal back to President George W. Bush on Veterans Day, 2018, becoming the first-ever military family member to return a war award to a U.S. president.

Bannerman has worked relentlessly to expand the reach of her message. She has written more than eighty articles and given over seven hundred interviews. She will be highlighted in a 2024 documentary about the human toll of war. from the perspectives of veterans, veterans' families, and those who fought against the Iraq War.

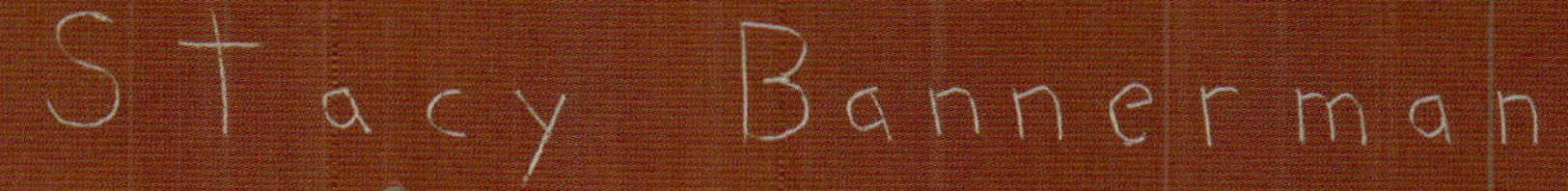

Stacy Bannerman

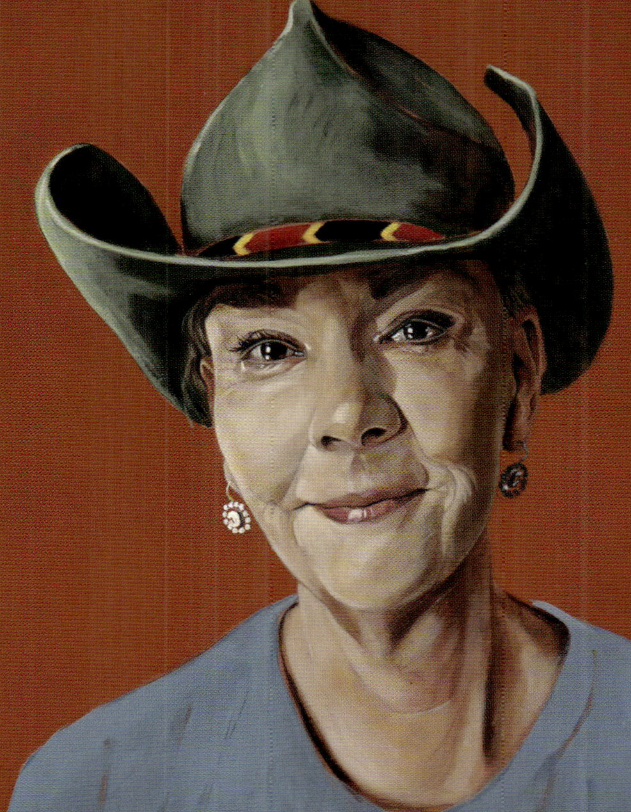

If we have a spiritual, moral, and humanitarian
mandate to alleviate suffering, then surely we are
ordained not to inflict it.

Medea Benjamin

Human rights advocate, antiwar activist, author; b. 1952

It is our responsibility as global citizens to learn to communicate with those we are taught to see as enemies.
For it is only when we understand each other, love each other, and think of every man and woman as
our brother and sister that we will finally be on our way to ending war.

Medea Benjamin was born Susan Benjamin. In college she changed her name to Medea after the complex figure from Greek mythology. She holds master degrees in public health and economics and has spent over forty years advocating for human rights around the world. Benjamin worked for ten years in Latin America and Africa as an economist and nutritionist for the United Nations Food and Agriculture Organization and the World Health Organization, among others, and lived for five years in Cuba. She is the author of ten books, beginning with *Bridging the Global Gap: A Handbook to Linking Citizens of the First and Third Worlds* (1989), coauthored with Andrea Freedman, and, most recently, *War in the Ukraine: Making Sense of a Senseless Conflict* (2022), coauthored with Nicolas J. S. Davies.

In 1988, Benjamin, her husband, Kevin Danaher, and Kirsten Moller cofounded Global Exchange, an organization dedicated to promoting fair trade practices, where environmental concerns and fair wages for producing goods take precedence over corporate profits. From the beginning, they fought against sweatshops, then helped organize the 1999 protests in Seattle against World Trade Organization policies. Global Exchange has continued over the past thirty-five years to envision and promote peaceful "people centered globalization."

After the attacks on September 11, 2001, Benjamin's activism took on a different tone and color; she cofounded CODEPINK: Women for Peace, a "women-run, women-led peace organization" whose activities range from meeting with members of Congress to dressing in pink surgical scrubs, handing out "prescriptions for peace." Their approach is inventive, often playful, and always in pink, but their goal for peace is serious. Their acts of civil disobedience can be confrontational and often involve members being arrested. After more than twenty years, CODEPINK thrives as a vital antiwar organization, with local affiliates across the country, from CODEPINK San Francisco to Divest Chattanooga.

In 2000, Benjamin ran for a California U.S. Senate seat on the Green Party ticket. She helped to bring groups together to form the United for Peace and Justice coalition. With initiatives too numerous to detail, she has opposed war on multiple fronts—including Gaza, Iraq, Afghanistan, Ukraine—and advocated extensively against drone warfare. For these continuous extraordinary efforts spanning several decades, she has received many honors, including the Martin Luther King, Jr. Peace Prize, the U.S. Peace Memorial Foundation's Peace Prize, the Gandhi Peace Award, and the Nuclear Age Peace Foundation's Peace Leadership Award.

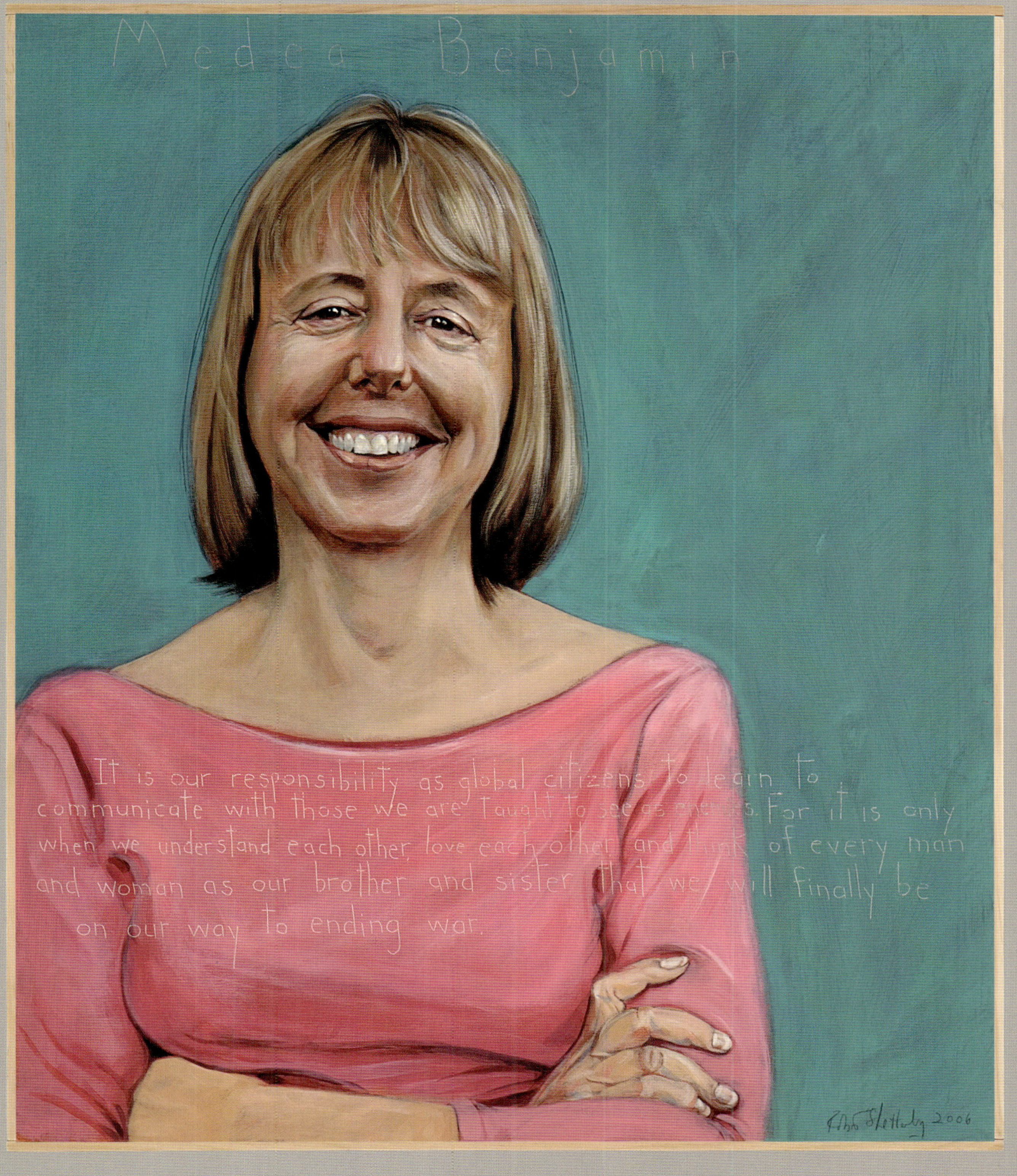

Medea Benjamin
It is our responsibility as global citizens to learn to communicate with those we are taught to see as enemies. For it is only when we understand each other, love each other and think of every man and woman as our brother and sister that we will finally be on our way to ending war.
Robert Shetterly 2006

Philip Berrigan

Civil rights, peace, antinuclear activist; b. 1923, d. 2002

*I see little difference between the world inside prison gates and the world outside.
A million million walls can't protect us, because the real dangers—militarism, greed,
economic inequality, fascism, police brutality—lie outside, not inside, prison walls.*

Philip Berrigan was no stranger to the prison system, having spent eleven years of his life in jail. At one time, Berrigan and his brother Daniel were on the FBI's Ten Most Wanted list for destruction of government property and other acts of vandalism committed in protest of the Vietnam War.

An internationally renowned American peace activist, Christian anarchist, and former Roman Catholic priest, Berrigan devoted his life to breaking down "prison walls" in order to expose and oppose American militarism, the use of nuclear weapons, social inequalities, avarice, and police brutality.

In 1943, after one semester at St. Michael's College in Toronto, Berrigan was drafted to fight in World War II. After the war, he graduated from the College of the Holy Cross, in Worcester, Massachusetts. Deeply affected by his exposure to the violence of war and the racism of boot camp in the South, he entered the Josephite Fathers' seminary in Newburgh, New York, a religious society of priests dedicated to serving Americans of African descent. He began marching for desegregation and participating in sit-ins and bus boycotts. He was ordained a priest in 1955. In 1973, Berrigan married Elizabeth McAlister, a nun; the Pope excommunicated the couple for marrying, and Berrigan left the priesthood.

In the 1960s, Berrigan took radical steps to bring attention to the antiwar movement. In 1967, he and three others—called the Baltimore Four— poured blood on Baltimore Selective Service records at the Customs House. As they waited for the police to arrive, the group passed out Bibles. Berrigan calmly lectured draft board employees, saying, "This sacrificial and constructive act is meant to protest the pitiful waste of American and Vietnamese blood in Indochina." He was sentenced to six years in prison.

In 1968, after his release on bail, Berrigan decided to repeat the Baltimore protest. The Catonsville Nine walked into the draft board of Catonsville, Maryland, removed 378 draft records, and burned them outside the building. He was sentenced to three and a half years in prison.

Together with a loosely affiliated group calling itself the Catholic Left, Berrigan planned or inspired dozens of other nonviolent actions between 1968 and 1975 in protest of the Vietnam War and the military-industrial complex.

In 1980, Berrigan, his brother Daniel, and six others started what became known as the Plowshares movement. Entering the General Electric Nuclear Missile Re-entry Division in King of Prussia, Pennsylvania, where warhead nose cones were manufactured, the activists hammered on two nose cones, poured blood on documents, and offered prayers for peace. They were arrested and initially charged with over ten felony and misdemeanor counts. After nearly ten years of trials and appeals, the Plowshares Eight were resentenced and paroled for close to two years in consideration of time already served in prison. Berrigan's final Plowshares action was in December 1999, when he and others banged on warplanes in an antiwar protest at the Warfield Air National Guard Base in Middle River, Maryland. Convicted of malicious destruction of property and sentenced to thirty months in prison, he was released December 14, 2001. Philip Berigan died in 2002 at the age of seventy-nine.

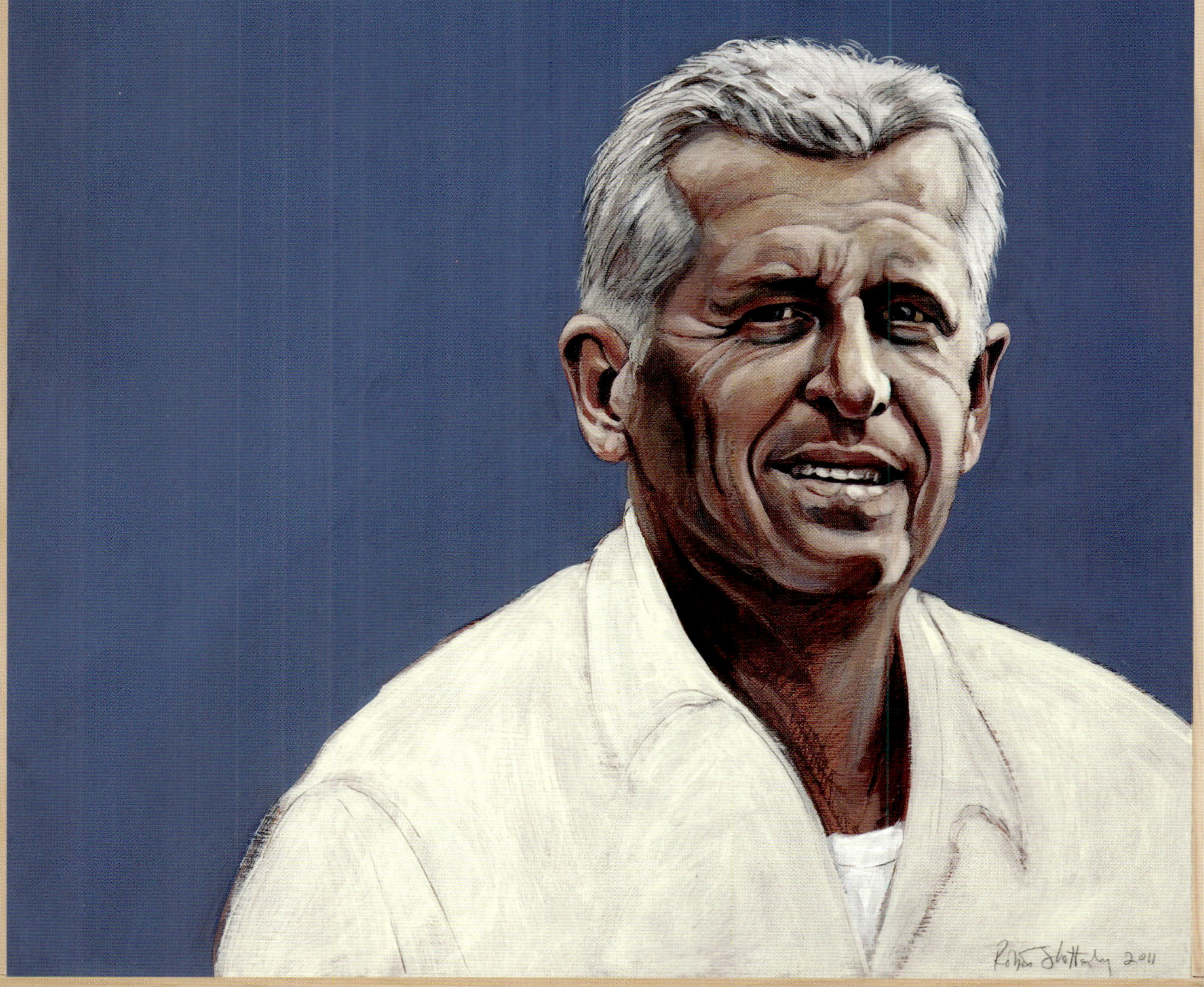

I see little difference between the world inside prison gates,
and the world outside. A million million prison walls can't protect us
because the real dangers — militarism, greed, economic inequality,
fascism, police brutality — lie outside, not inside, prison walls.

Philip Berrigan

Father Roy Bourgeois

Peace and human rights activist, former Catholic priest; b. 1938

Just down the road here is a school, the School of the Americas. It's a combat school. Most of the courses revolve around what they call "counter insurgency warfare." Who are the insurgents? We have to ask that question. They are the poor. They are the people in Latin America who call for reform. They are the landless peasants who are hungry. They are health care workers, human rights advocates, labor organizers. They become the insurgents. They're seen as El Enemigo, the Enemy. And they are those who become the targets of those who learn their lessons at the School of the Americas.

In the quote above, Roy Bourgeois, former Catholic priest and founder of the School of the Americas Watch (SOAW), describes the military training ground—now called the Western Hemisphere Institute for Security Cooperation (WHINSEC)—at Fort Benning in Georgia. WHINSEC trains military and police officers from Latin America and the United States in torture, execution, and other forms of coercion. Bourgeois's work reveals the truth about the programs taught there and aims to close what is often referred to as the "School of Assassins."

Bourgeois was born in 1938 in Louisiana's Cajun country. Growing up in a conservative working-class family, he attended public school and a state university, playing football and graduating with a degree in geology, hoping to make his fortune in the oil fields.

Duty to God and country called Bourgeois to the navy. His experiences in Vietnam changed the course of his life. As bombs exploded, fires raged, and napalm burned villages, Bourgeois discovered Vietnam's people and culture. He spent weekends volunteering at a Catholic orphanage, where he witnessed the magnitude of the suffering generated by war.

Bourgeois returned home to a hero's welcome and received the Purple Heart, but he already knew that he wanted to shift his attention to peacemaking. In 1968, he began studies to become a Maryknoll missionary priest. For protesting the Vietnam War, he spent the first of what would be a total of four years in jail. In 1972, he was sent to Bolivia, where he worked in poor communities for five years before being deported from the country for speaking out against human rights violations and organizing to overthrow Bolivia's dictator, Gen. Hugo Banzer.

Bourgeois became involved again in Latin American events when, in 1980, three Catholic nuns and a lay missionary, two of whom were friends of Bourgeois, were raped and killed in El Salvador and Archbishop Oscar Romero was assassinated. Nine years later, six Jesuit priests were massacred along with their housekeeper and the housekeeper's daughter.

When Bourgeois discovered links between these events and the School of the Americas, he became an outspoken critic of U.S. Latin American policy. He rented an apartment near the entrance to the school, dubbed it "Casa Romero," and founded the SOAW. In November 1990, the first anniversary of the Jesuit massacre, SOAW staged a public protest; Father Bourgeois was arrested and jailed. The SOAW protests and other antiwar activities continued.

When Bourgeois participated in a woman's ordination ceremony in Lexington, Kentucky, he was excommunicated from the Catholic Church. At the ordination, he stated, "No matter how hard we may try to justify discrimination, in the end it is always immoral." In April 2022, Bourgeois released the book *Male Supremacy in the Catholic Church: An Insider's View.* He believes that "the truth cannot be silenced. It simply cannot be silenced."

Just down the road here is a school, the School of the Americas. It's a combat school. Most of the courses revolve around what they call "counter insurgency warfare." Who are the insurgents? We have to ask that question. They are the poor. They are the people in Latin America who call for reform. They are the landless peasants who are hungry. They are health care workers, human rights advocats, labor organizers. They become the insurgents, they're seen as "El Enemigo," the Enemy. And they are those who become the targets of those who learn their lessons at the School of the Americas.

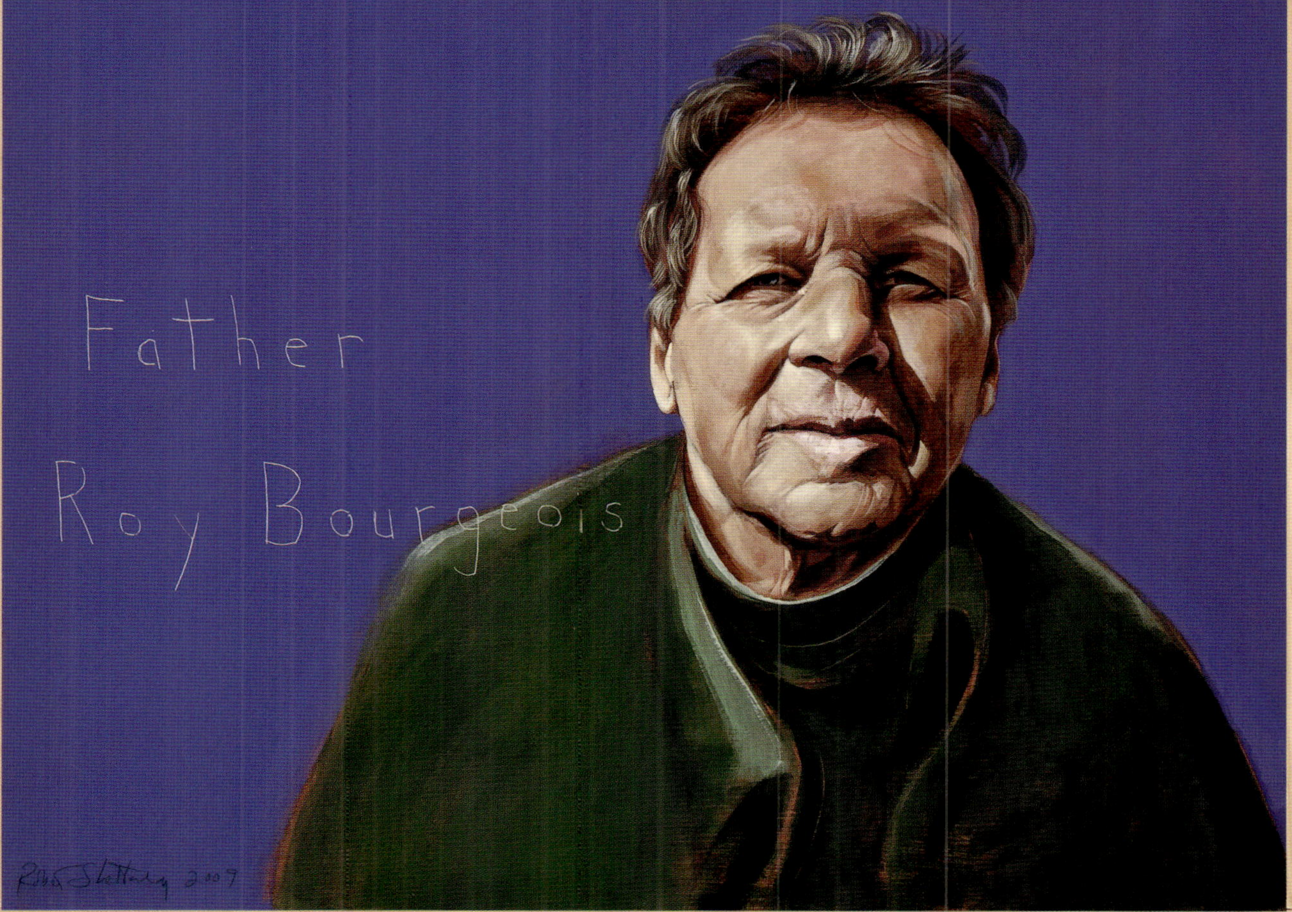

Betty Burkes

Peace educator; b. 1942

How do we redefine ourselves to be motivated to connect and share rather than shop and consume, replenish rather than extract? How does this transformation happen? . . . At the heart of this transformation is not technology but relationships, tens of millions of people working toward restoration and social justice.

Betty Burkes has come to understand the world around her through relationships and community. She believes peace is achievable through the hard work of honest dialogue and self-reflection.

Burkes grew up in a working-class family in Ohio. After college, she joined the Peace Corps and taught in Ethiopia. She received a master's degree in early childhood education at the University of California, Berkeley. Later, she lived in England for many years, where she studied art and dance and taught at the American School in London. In 1986, she returned to the United States and opened two programs on Cape Cod—Summer Center, then Montessori Paradise—where she explored the world with preschool children, developing their respect for nature, relational skills, and sense of responsibility, as well as teaching arts, crafts, and music.

In the 1980s, Burkes joined the Women's International League for Peace and Freedom (WILPF) and served on its national board and as U.S. Section president. Interviewed about WILPF on the television program *Enviro Close-Up,* Burkes discussed the "culture of power" in the United States. She suggested that by investigating our country's history of violence and deception, we can better understand the attitudes and values that shape our lives and form the basis of our national policies. She believes that the way to effect change is to educate ourselves, open our hearts to the realities of those whose lives and views are different from our own, and join forces with others.

From 2002 to 2006, Burkes worked for the Hague Appeal for Peace. The organization operates in collaboration with the UN Department of Disarmament Affairs to abolish war and establish peace as a human right. There she served as Peace Education Program coordinator on projects in Albania, Cambodia, Niger, and Peru, where she worked with in-country partners to design peace education curricula for national school systems and programs to promote local conflict-resolution skills.

Burkes coordinated programs for Kids Rethink New Orleans Schools. In the aftermath of Hurricane Katrina, the Rethink project encouraged middle school youth to participate actively in the reimagining of New Orleans schools. The students developed leadership and critical-thinking skills and worked to build community. Closer to home, Burkes serves on the steering committee for CORE, the Boston area–based Coalition of Racial Equality in Mental Health, and as board chair of the Cambridge Insight Meditation Center.

Betty Burkes believes in a "beloved community," where all life is valued and human interactions are guided by equality and compassion. She believes that structures of power can be transformed through nonviolence and education that promotes inquiry and investigation, patience, and love. Wherever she is, Burkes works locally for global change, racial and community justice, a healthy environment, and peace building.

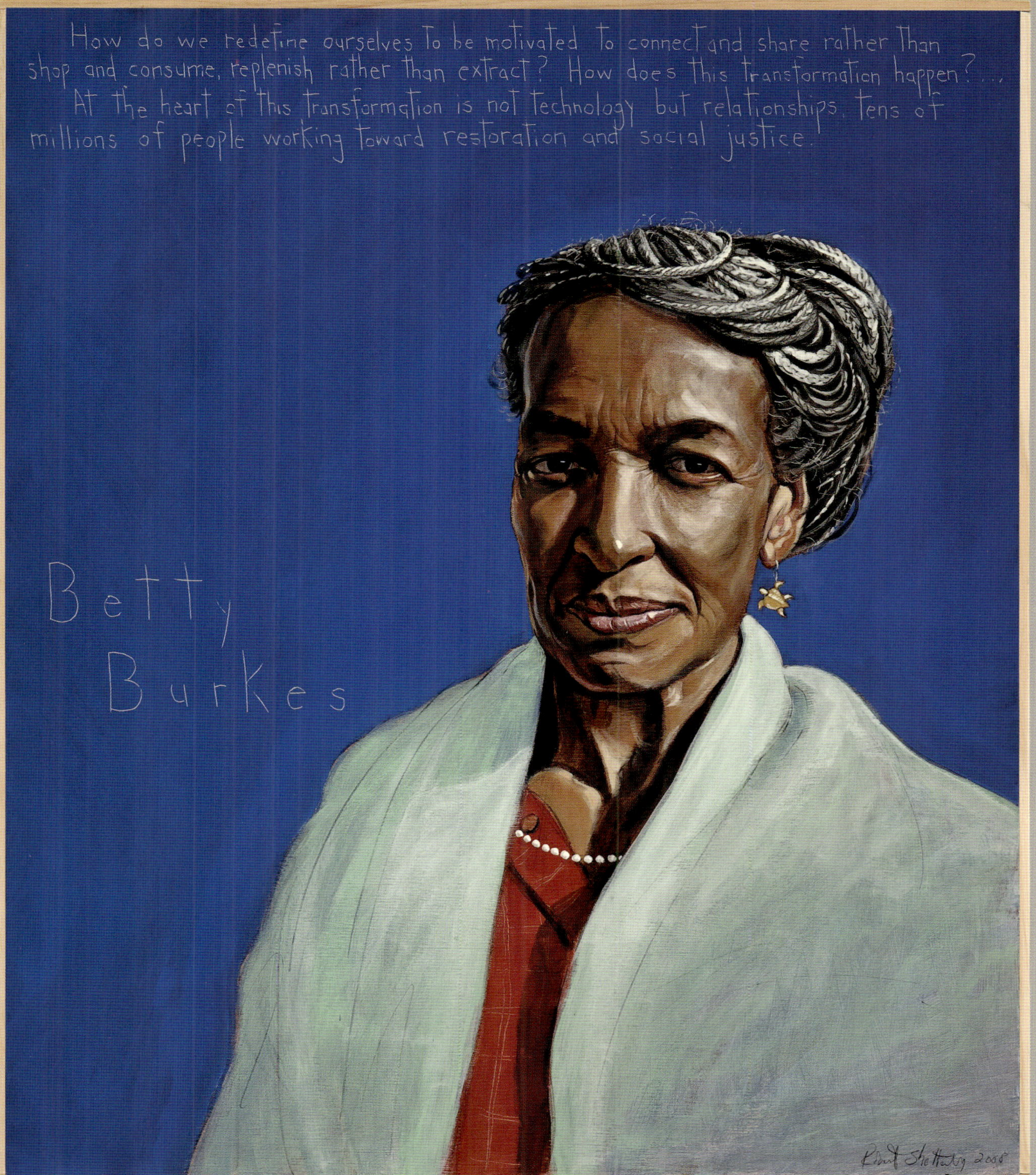

How do we redefine ourselves To be motivated to connect and share rather Than
shop and consume, replenish rather than extract? How does this transformation happen?...
At the heart of this transformation is not technology but relationships, tens of
millions of people working toward restoration and social justice.

Betty
Burkes

Major General Smedley Butler

Major general in the U.S. Marine Corp, antiwar activist; b. 1881, d. 1940

I served in all commissioned ranks from second lieutenant to Major General. And during that period I spent most of my time being a high-class muscle man for Big Business, for Wall Street and for the bankers. In short, I was a racketeer for capitalism. I suspected I was just part of the racket all the time. Now I am sure of it.

At the time of his death, Maj. Gen. Smedley Darlington Butler, also known as "the Fighting Quaker," was the most decorated marine in U.S. history; he was the only person to have been awarded a Marine Corps Brevet Medal and the Medal of Honor twice, for separate military actions. He had also become an unrelenting voice against the business of war.

Raised by prominent Quaker parents, Butler defied his pacifist lineage by joining the Marine Corps just before his seventeenth birthday. He served in Honduras, Nicaragua, Mexico, and Haiti. Butler was known for his leadership and commitment to the welfare of the men under his command. He rose quickly through the ranks to become, at age forty-eight, one of the youngest major generals.

Prior to World War II, Butler spoke out against what he saw as admiration for fascism and for Italy's leader, Benito Mussolini. He was punished for telling an unfavorable story about Mussolini but avoided court-martial by accepting a reprimand. Because of his rank, he was able to write his own reprimand, and he never apologized to Mussolini.

Butler retired from the military in 1931. By then, he was beginning to question U.S. involvement in foreign conflicts, thinking of himself as a cog in the imperialist war machine. In a booklet titled *War Is a Racket*, Butler wrote, "In the World War [I] a mere handful garnered the profits of the conflict. At least 21,000 new millionaires and billionaires were made in the United States during the World War. . . . How many of these war millionaires shouldered a rifle? . . . The public shoulders the bill. And what is this bill? . . . Newly placed gravestones. Mangled bodies. Shattered minds. . . . For a great many years, as a soldier, I had a suspicion that war was a racket; not until I retired to civil life did I fully realize it. Now that I see the international war clouds gathering, as they are today, I must face it and speak out."

War Is a Racket grew out of a series of speeches Butler gave to whatever group was willing to hear his views. Although he faced criticism, Butler was steadfast in his beliefs about war, U.S. imperialism, and a growing pro-fascist movement. He spoke frankly and honestly about his experiences and opinions and was very popular with the American public.

In 1934, Butler went before the House Committee on Un-American Activities to expose a conspiracy against the government. He had been recruited by a group of wealthy pro-fascists who had hoped to use him in a coup against President Franklin D. Roosevelt. He went along, gathering intelligence about the plot, and took it to Congress. Butler's assertions were not aggressively pursued, and the matter was largely dismissed. However, an internal report to Congress from HUAC confirmed the veracity of the plot.

The Boston, Massachusetts, chapter of Veterans for Peace is named the Smedley D. Butler Brigade, and he is featured in the documentary *The Corporation* (2003).

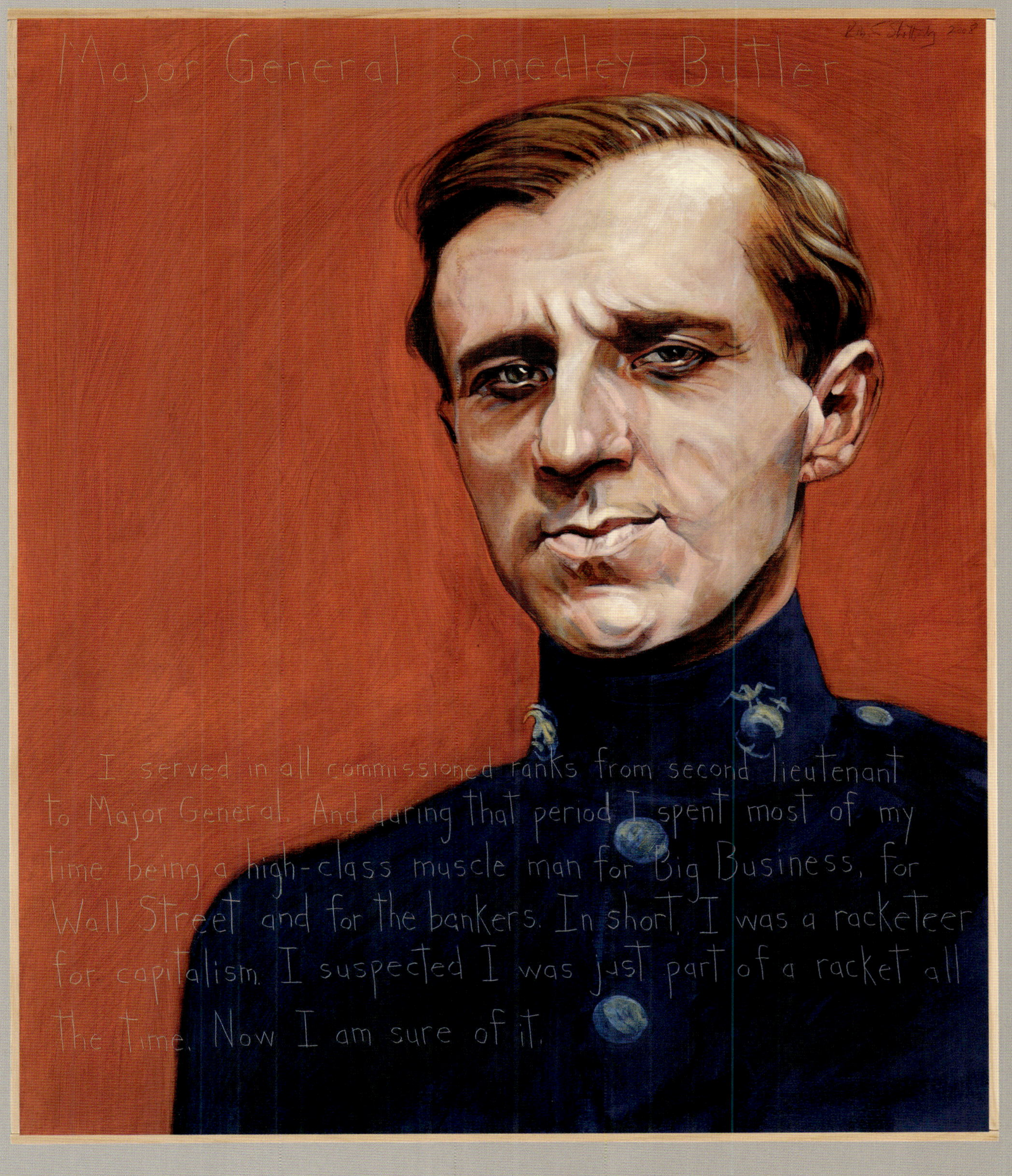

Major General Smedley Butler

I served in all commissioned ranks from second lieutenant
to Major General. And during that period I spent most of my
time being a high-class muscle man for Big Business, for
Wall Street and for the bankers. In short, I was a racketeer
for capitalism. I suspected I was just part of a racket all
the time. Now I am sure of it.

Paul K. Chappell

Army captain, peace activist, writer; b. 1980

When people in a democracy are not educated in the art of living—to strengthen their conscience, compassion, and ability to question and think critically—they can be easily manipulated by fear and propaganda. A democracy is only as wise as its citizens, and a democracy of ignorant citizens can be as dangerous as a dictatorship.

Paul K. Chappell is the son of a Korean mother and an African American father whose thirty years of military service included combat duty in Korea and Vietnam. Following in his father's military footsteps, Chappell graduated from West Point in 2002 and served as a captain in Iraq.

While on active duty, Chappell wrote two books, *Will War Ever End?: A Soldier's Vision of Peace for the 21st Century* (2009) and *The End of War: How Waging Peace Can Save Humanity, Our Planet, and Our Future* (2010). Since then, he has continued to explore the themes of war and peace, with four more published books and a seventh, *The Transcendent Mystery: A New Paradigm for Understanding Peace, Trauma, Technology, and the Human Condition,* yet to be released.

Chappell's books offer compelling insights on how we might end war. Based on his personal experience, military training, and research into human nature and the myths that perpetuate war, Chappell avoids blaming any particular political group; his ideas have found traction with liberals, conservatives, veterans, and civilians.

It's too simple to say that Chappell is a soldier turned peace leader. Growing up in a violent household in Alabama, his character was forged by violence, rage, and racism. Chappell's struggle with war and peace began at the age of four, when his shell-shocked father started beating him. Chappell grew up believing that humans are by nature violent and that war is inevitable. As a cadet at West Point,

he learned that neither of these beliefs was true. And as a soldier in Iraq, he decided to dedicate his life to helping others understand why.

Chappell believes that peace activists must be highly trained in the art of waging peace, just as soldiers are highly trained for war. He also believes—like Gandhi, Martin Luther King, Jr., and James Lawson—that many of the warrior ideals are vital for a nonviolent campaign to be effective. These warrior ideals include courage, discipline, determination, resilience, strategic thinking, selflessness, teamwork, and striving for the common good rather than personal glory.

In 2017, Chapell founded the Peace Literacy Institute, where he serves as executive director. The institute offers to schools around the world free peace literacy curricula and low-cost teacher training. The institute is also a leader in the global campaign for peace literacy to become recognized as a universal human right.

Despite the many problems of our era, Chappell believes that the twenty-first century is an exciting and hopeful time, when a new "peaceful revolution" has the potential to reduce war and injustice around the world. He says, "The peaceful revolution is a revolution of mind, heart, and spirit. But it is also a scientific revolution. . . . The peaceful revolution will create a paradigm shift that changes how we see war, peace, our responsibility to the planet, our kinship with each other, and what it means to be human."

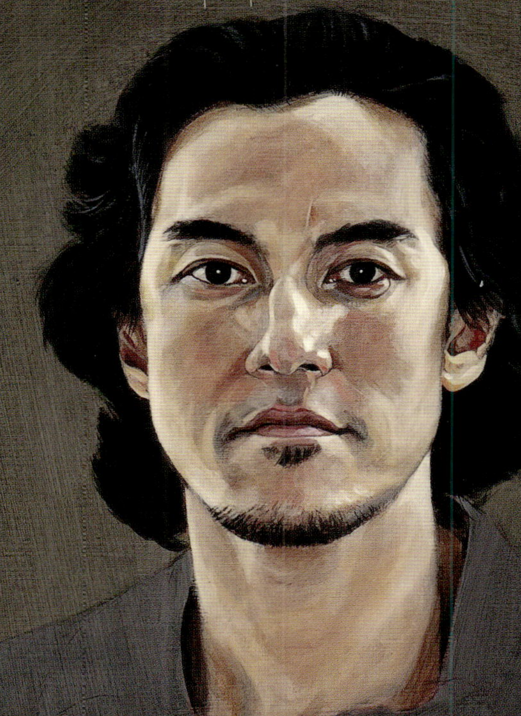

Paul K. Chappell

When people in a democracy are not   educated in the art of
living — to strengthen their conscience, compassion, and ability to
question and think critically — they can be easily manipulated by
fear and propaganda. A democracy is only as wise as its citizens,
and a democracy of ignorant citizens can be as dangerous
as a dictatorship.

Ramsey Clark

U.S. attorney general, justice advocate; b. 1927, d. 2021

The press rendered First Amendment protection meaningless because its wealthy owners uncritically supported the government as it destroyed Iraq. TV coverage . . . was more a long-running commercial for war, weapons systems, and militarism than for news reporting. . . . The tragedy of our time is that we celebrate the power of violence and not the pity of it.

Born in Dallas in 1927, Attorney General Ramsey Clark grew up in a family steeped in Texas culture and politics. His father, Tom Clark, taught him the ways of the outdoorsman and the values of the rugged individualist. On weekends they camped, fished, and hunted. Tom's involvement in local politics had Ramsey attending rallies and speeches, hanging posters, and handing out flyers. Tom Clark's work as one of the few local attorneys willing to represent African Americans had a profound impact on his son.

Clark's early career followed expectations. He joined the Marine Corps in 1945 and served as a courier in postwar Europe. He earned three degrees—a bachelor's, a master's, and a law degree—in four years. He married his college sweetheart, Georgia Welch, fathered two children, and returned to Dallas to become a partner in his uncle's law firm. On behalf of Safeway Stores, he argued his first case before the U.S. Supreme Court. Tom Clark, appointed to the Court in 1949, recused himself to avoid any appearance of a conflict of interest.

A political outsider in a state that leaned more and more conservative, Clark stayed away from Texas politics. At the same time, he became bored with corporate law. "I got tired of fighting over other people's money," he explained. Then came an opportunity, in the form of John F. Kennedy. In 1961, Ramsey became the Department of Justice's assistant attorney general for the Lands Division. Later, Bobby Kennedy sent Clark to the South to enforce federal integration orders. Moving his way up the government ladder, he was appointed Lyndon Johnson's attorney general in 1967. His years in public service would change the course of his life.

After leaving office in 1969, Clark began the second stage of his career. He first wrote *Crime in America*, a book excoriating the correctional system, proposing a systemic overhaul that favored rehabilitation over punishment. Clark then went on a fact-finding trip to North Vietnam. He returned from his journey an outspoken critic of U.S. intervention overseas.

He took a job with a progressive New York law firm, where he focused his energy on pro bono cases, defending antiwar activists, prison rioters, and death row inmates. He joined the board of Amnesty International and worked with Coretta Scott King to establish a national holiday in honor of her slain husband. He ran for the U.S. Senate and lost.

In 1991, Clark traveled to Iraq to view the devastation wrought by Operation Desert Storm. He documented violations of international law and war crimes by the U.S. government and witnessed the devastation of sanctions on the people of Iraq. In 2004, Clark joined the Saddam Hussein's defense team, hoping to hold the tribunal accountable to the laws and spirit of the Geneva Accords and the U.S. Constitution.

Clark's willingness to provide legal advice and representation to those on the fringes of society and dubbed enemies of the United States brought him both admiration and disdain. To some, he was a voice of truth in a system defined by hypocrisy. Others saw him as anti-American. A man of strong ideals and few words, Clark would provide a simple response: "Democracy is not a spectator sport."

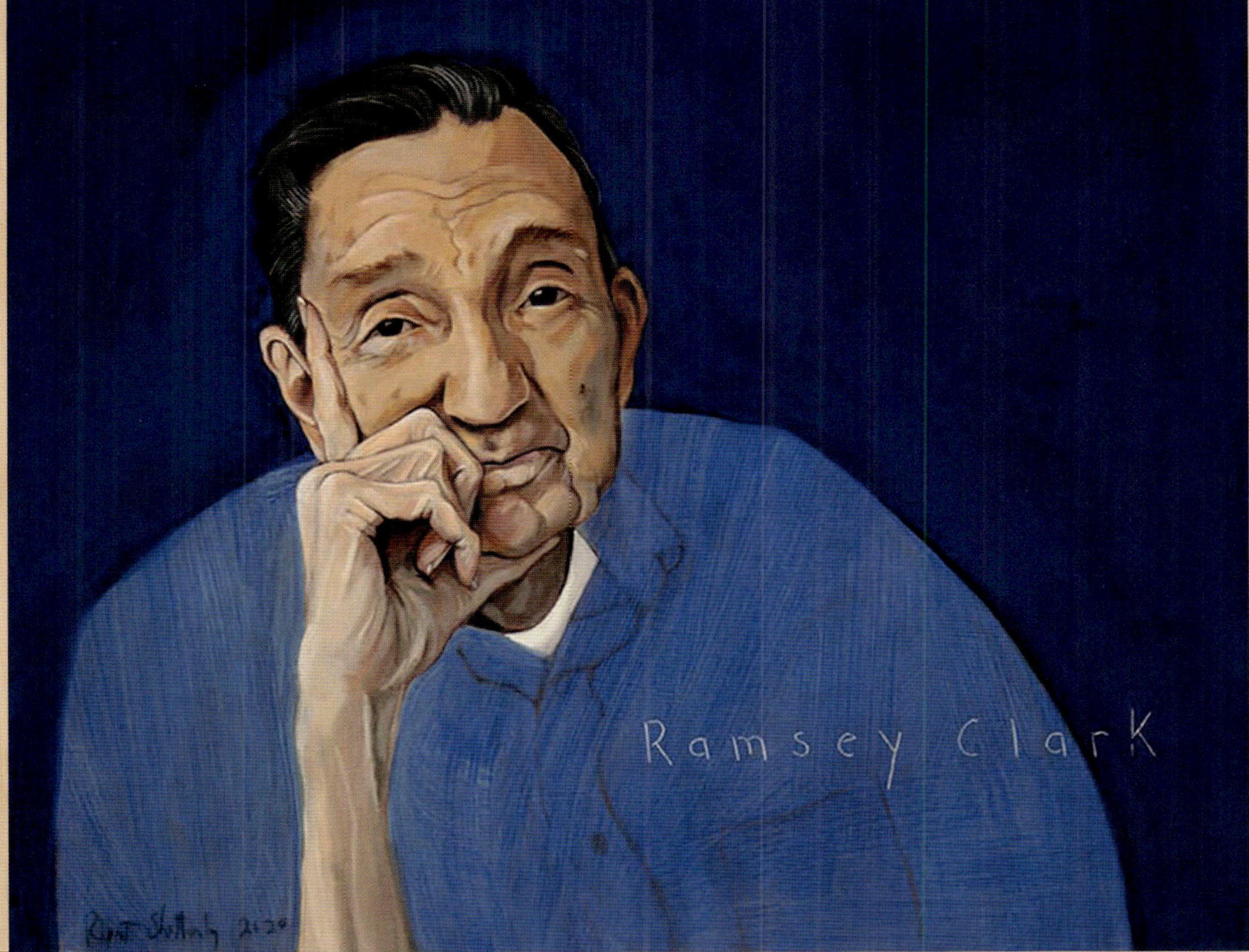

The press rendered First Amendment protection meaningless because its wealthy owners uncritically supported the government as it destroyed Iraq. TV coverage... was more a long running commercial for war, weapons systems, and militarism than news reporting... The tragedy of our time is that we celebrate the power of violence and not the pity of it.
Ramsey Clark

Charlie Clements

Writer, peace and human rights advocate; b. 1945

Activists in the U.S. are like the "tank man" in Tiananmen Square in China. We have always had to jump in front of this ship of state to keep it on a self-correcting course. Whether the issue was slavery, labor rights, women's suffrage, civil rights, Vietnam, Central America, or Iraq, it is the determined protests of those who will settle for nothing less than justice or peace that have altered the course of history. The moral arc of the universe doesn't bend toward justice by gravity.

During the civil war in El Salvador, Charlie Clements worked as a physician in rural villages that were bombed, rocketed, or strafed daily by their own government. One day a peasant asked, "Why don't you carry a weapon like the other doctors?" Clements explained that after the Vietnam War, he became a Quaker. The peasant shook his head in disdain, saying, "You gringos are always concerned about violence done with machetes or machine guns." The man had been required to feed the hacienda owner's animals and get them veterinary care, while watching his own children go hungry and die. "You will never understand violence or nonviolence until you understand the violence to the spirit from watching helplessly as your children suffer."

Clements wasn't always committed to nonviolence. He was a Distinguished Graduate of the Air Force Academy, and after training as a pilot, he volunteered for service in Vietnam. After nine months in Southeast Asia, he concluded that the war was immoral and refused to fly further missions. He was placed in a psychiatric ward and discharged with a 10 percent mental disability.

With 90 percent of his mental facilities still intact, he attended medical school. Treating patients led him to understand that exploitation, poverty, and injustice were often the underlying reasons for sickness or injuries.

In 1980, while working in a clinic for undocumented farmworkers, Clements heard stories from Salvadoran refugees about death squads killing teachers, physicians, and priests. When the United States began sending helicopters and military advisers there, he feared that another Vietnam War was unfolding. He volunteered his skills as a physician in an area controlled by the FMLN guerrillas. Upon returning from El Salvador, Clements testified in Congress and crisscrossed the country, speaking about the brutality of U.S. foreign policy. He led congressional delegations to the region and raised millions of dollars for humanitarian assistance. *Witness to War* (1984) is the account of his journey of conscience from Vietnam to El Salvador

When the civil war ended in 1992, Clements was a special guest at the signing of the Chapultepec Peace Accords in Mexico City. Seventeen years later, he was a guest at the inauguration of Mauricio Funes, the first FMLN candidate to win the presidency.

In 1997, as president of Physicians for Human Rights, Clements attended the signing of the treaty to ban land mines and the Nobel Prize ceremony for the International Campaign to Ban Landmines (ICBL). Later he served as the president and CEO of the Unitarian Universalist Service Committee and director of the Carr Institute for Human Rights.

When asked what sustains him, Clements offers a quote from the Talmud: "Do not be daunted by the enormity of the world's grief. Love mercy now. Walk humbly now. Do justly now. You are not obligated to complete the work, but neither are you free to abandon it."

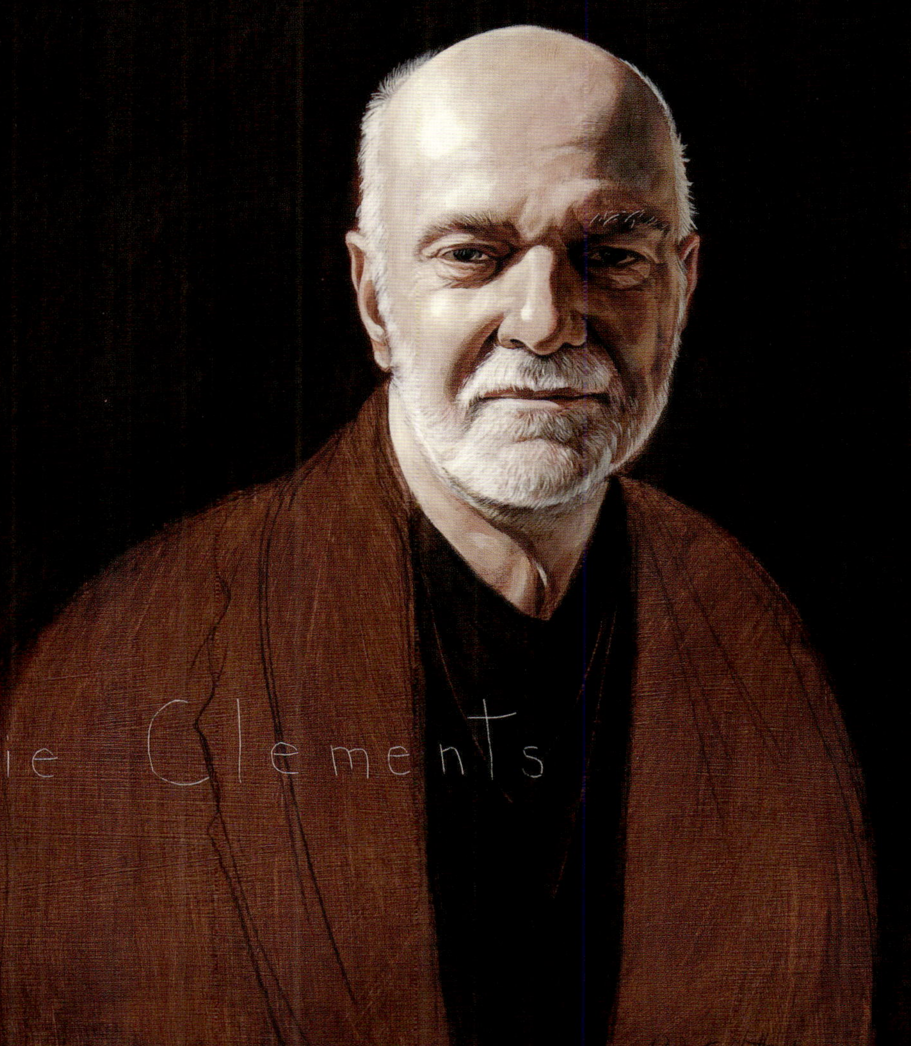

Activists in the U.S. are like the "tank man" in Tiananmen Square in China. We have always had to jump in front of this ship of state to keep it on a self-correcting course. Whether the issue was slavery, labor rights, women's sufferage, civil rights, Vietnam, Central America, or Iraq, it is the determined protests of those who will settle for nothing less than justice or peace that have altered the course of history.

The moral arc of the universe doesn't bend toward justice by gravity.

Charlie Clements

William Sloane Coffin

Clergyman, social activist; b. 1924, d. 2006

*The war against Iraq is as disastrous as it is unnecessary; perhaps in terms of its wisdom,
purpose and motives, the worst war in American history. . . . Our military men and women . . . were not
called to defend America but rather to attack Iraq. They were not called to die for, but rather to kill for, their country.
What more unpatriotic thing could we have asked of our sons and daughters . . . ?*

For more than forty years, William Sloane Coffin spoke with prophetic zeal on matters of war and peace, social justice, and religious faith.

His early years—birth in New York City, childhood in Carmel, California, musical studies in Paris, and education at a New England preparatory school—suggest a world of almost limitless opportunity. Wartime enlistment in the army and four years of active duty suggest his readiness to engage with history in the making.

After the war, he earned a degree at Yale, enrolled in theological seminary, and then worked for three years in the Central Intelligence Agency. Coffin returned to theology in 1953, earning his bachelor of divinity degree from Yale. He was ordained a Presbyterian minister and attained national prominence during his seventeen years as chaplain at Yale. In 1977, he became senior minister of Riverside Church in New York City. Ten years later he resigned in order to lead SANE/Freeze (later renamed Peace Action). At the end of his life, he lived in Vermont, where he completed a book of reflections on his faith, *Credo* (2004).

Coffin's immersion in the controversial moral issues of his generation began in 1960 with international relief work. The following year, he helped train the first group of Peace Corps volunteers in Puerto Rico. Civil rights dominated the early 1960s; Coffin was one of the Freedom Riders who challenged segregation laws by riding interstate buses in the South. He was arrested on several occasions. Like his fellow clergyman, Martin Luther King, Jr., Coffin turned his attention in the mid-1960s to the escalating U.S. military involvement in Vietnam, which he actively protested. He cofounded the Americans for Re-appraisal of Far Eastern Policy and joined other religious leaders in forming the National Emergency Committee of Clergy Concerned About Vietnam. With Dr. Benjamin Spock and others, he was charged and convicted with conspiracy to aid draft resisters, a verdict overturned on appeal in 1970. Coffin's memoir, *Once to Every Man* (1977), details this period of civil rights advocacy and peace activism.

Coffin's commitment to humanity sprang from his religious faith, and the core of his faith was love: "To show compassion for an individual without showing concern for the structures of society that make him an object of compassion is to be sentimental rather than loving."

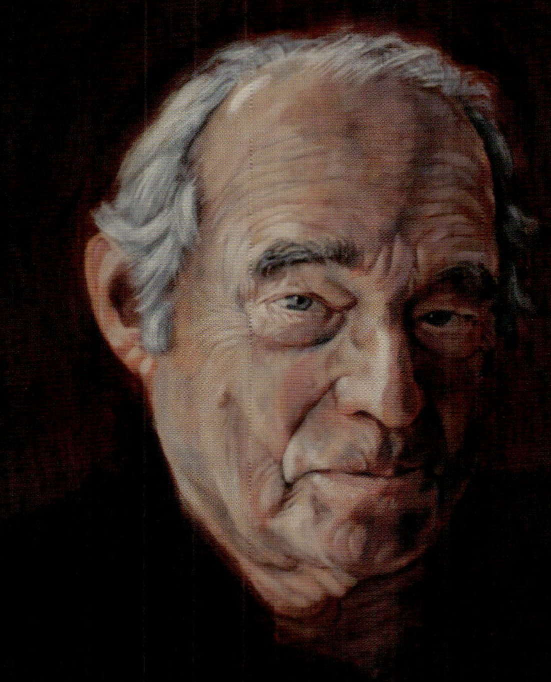

The war against Iraq is as disastrous as it is unnecessary; perhaps in terms of its wisdom, justice, purpose and motives, the worst war in American history... Our military men and women... were not called to defend America but rather to attack Iraq. They were not called to die for, but rather to kill for their country. What more unpatriotic thing could we have asked of our sons and daughters?

William Sloane Coffin

Rachel Corrie

Protester; b. 1979, d. 2003

The international media and our government are not going to tell us that we are effective, important, justified in our work, courageous, intelligent, valuable. We have to do that for each other, and one way we can do that is by continuing our work, visibly. . . . people without privilege will be doing this work no matter what, because they are working for their lives. We can work with them, and they know that we work with them, or we can leave them to do this work themselves and curse us for our complicity in killing them.

Rachel Corrie was a twenty-three-year-old activist whose life ended abruptly on March 16, 2003, while she was working as a protester in the Gaza Strip. She grew up in Olympia, Washington, attended Capital High School and then The Evergreen State College. While in college, Corrie joined the Olympia Movement for Justice and Peace, and later, the International Solidarity Movement (ISM).

The ISM, founded in 2001, looks worldwide for people to help with their nonviolent protests against the Israeli military in the West Bank. The organization seeks to pressure Israel and its Israeli Defense Forces (IDF) into ending its occupation of Palestinian lands, using a number of nonviolent resistance tactics, such as violating Israeli curfews imposed in Palestinian areas, removing roadblocks placed by the IDF to isolate one village from another, and blocking military tanks and bulldozers.

Corrie went to Rafah in the Gaza Strip in January 2003 and received two days of nonviolent resistance training to assist in ISM activities. She was horrified at the destruction she found there. Homes were destroyed and people detained and killed on a daily basis. Rachel recorded what she observed and how she felt in letters and emails to her family. In one email, she wrote, "Now the Israeli army has actually dug up the road to Gaza, and both of the major checkpoints are closed. This means that

Palestinians who want to go and register for their next quarter at university can't. People can't get to their jobs and those who are trapped on the other side can't get home; and internationals, who have a meeting tomorrow in the West Bank, won't make it."

In another email, Corrie wrote, "Just feel sick to my stomach a lot from being doted on all the time, very sweetly, by people who are facing doom. . . . Honestly, a lot of the time the sheer kindness of the people here, coupled with the overwhelming evidence of the willful destruction of their lives, makes it seem unreal to me."

Corrie's efforts to help the resistance movement cost her her life. She placed herself between a Caterpillar bulldozer and a local home, trying to prevent the IDF from demolishing the house. She was run over twice by the vehicle and killed.

After her death, The Rachel Corrie Foundation for Peace & Justice was founded to "support programs that foster connections between people, that build understanding, respect, and appreciation for differences, and that promote cooperation within and between local and global communities." Actor Alan Rickman and writer Katherine Viner put together a play based on Corrie's letters, journals, and emails called *My Name Is Rachel Corrie*. It played in London in 2005, and, after an initial postponement in the United States, had a limited run Off-Broadway in New York.

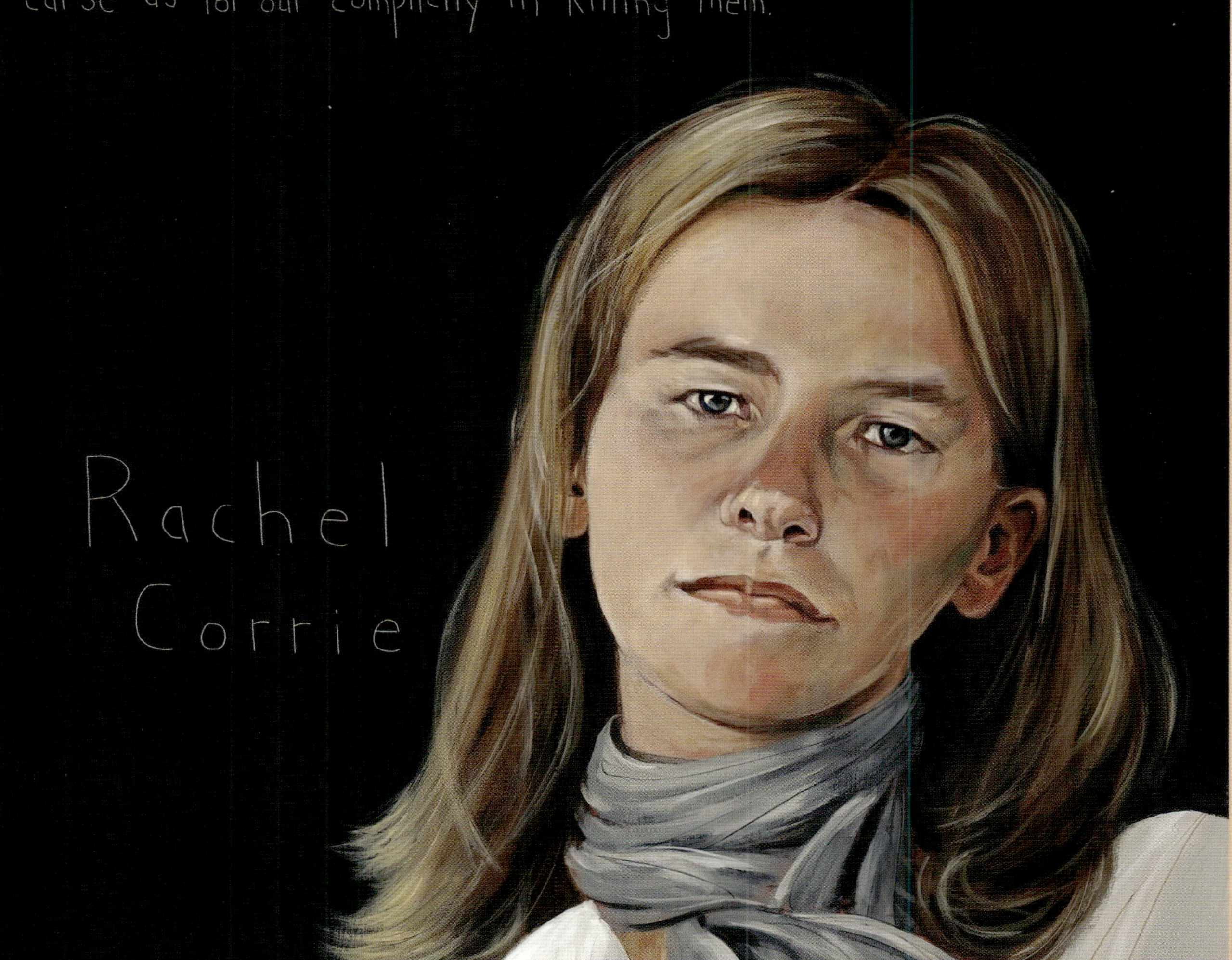

The international media and our government are not going to tell us that
we are effective, important, justified in our work, courageous, intelligent,
valuable. We have to do that for each other, and one way we can do that is
by continuing our work, visibly.
. . . people without privilege will be doing this work no matter what, because
they are working for their lives. We can work with them, and they know that
we work with them, or we can leave them to do this work themselves and
curse us for our complicity in killing them.

Rachel
Corrie

Frances Crowe

Peace activist; b. 1919, d. 2019

Once people believed in human sacrifice—not any more. Once people believed in slavery—not any more. Once people believed that women should not vote—not any more. In your lifetime I hope your children can say: Once people believed in war as the answer—not anymore.

On August 30, 2011, six women chained themselves to the front gate of the Vermont Yankee nuclear power plant. For their diminutive ninety-three-year-old leader, Frances Crowe, this was at least her twentieth action against the reactor. Later she told the Associated Press, "They're finally taking us seriously and they are taking us to trial. . . . But I know I haven't achieved what I am trying to achieve."

When she was a teenager in her hometown of Carthage, Missouri, Crowe blurted to her father that she was against killing and war. This revelation was prompted by the public hanging of a black prisoner at the local jail.

Her lifelong commitment to the antiwar movement began a few years later in 1945—after college, graduate school at Syracuse and Columbia, and a spell working in a laboratory that supported the war effort. She was ironing a place mat in the New Orleans apartment where she lived with her husband. "I heard on the radio that they dropped the bomb on Hiroshima. And I knew, with the description of what it was, that it was really bad. . . . So then I literally unplugged the iron and went out looking for a peace center in New Orleans." Although she didn't find one, she began reading about the history of nonviolence.

She and her husband, Tom, became connected with the Quakers, with whom she began organizing. Then in 1968, as her teenage sons approached draft age, she started the Northampton Draft Information Center, counseling thousands of young men on how to become conscientious objectors.

On International Women's Day in 1972, Crowe and a Women Against the War group went to the Westover Air Force Base in Chicopee, Massachusetts, dressed as Vietnamese women. They knelt to block the base's main gate, reading Vietnamese poetry aloud. An armed-bomber pilot home on R&R, Capt. Donald Dawson, who was sent to keep eye on them, was transformed. These were real people he was killing, he realized. He refused to return to active duty. When he was court-martialed, Crowe reached out to him to offer her support. He became the first American pilot during the Vietnam War to get an honorable discharge as a conscientious objector.

When the local public radio station declined to carry Amy Goodman's show, *Democracy Now!*, Crowe bought a transmitter and broadcast it herself— illegally. After running successful fund-raising campaigns in competition with the local stations, they agreed to negotiate. As a result, the University of Massachusetts Amherst radio station, WMUA, became the first college radio station in the country to broadcast *Democracy Now!*

A war tax resister, Crowe gave her tax savings to peacekeeping organizations and the local public schools. The Northampton, Massachusetts, police chief told a *Boston Globe* reporter before her death at age one hundred, "She's the ultimate liberal—a real icon of our community and a wonderful woman."

Crowe said, "I have a vision of a better world where people can live cooperatively, without violence, and that we would be able to feed the hungry, house the homeless, and provide shelter for people if we weren't spending so much money on war."

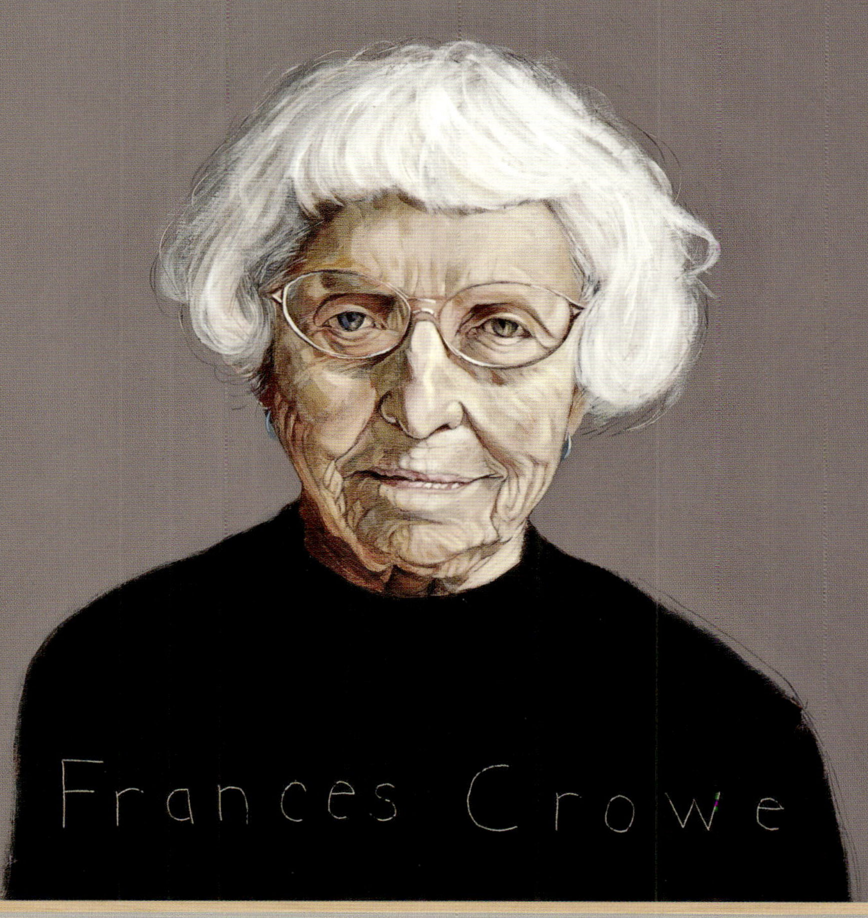

Once, people believed in human sacrifice — not any more. Once, people believed in slavery — not any more. Once, people believed that women should not vote — not any more. In your lifetime I hope your children can say: Once, people believed in war as the answer — not any more.
Frances Crowe

Dorothy Day

Social activist, journalist; b. 1897, d. 1980

The biggest mistake, sometimes, is to play things very safe in this life and end up being moral failures.

Dorothy Day was born in New York in 1897. After living in Chicago for most of her childhood, she attended the University of Illinois at Urbana-Champaign for two years, then returned to New York with her family in 1916. Her reading of such authors as Leo Tolstoy and Upton Sinclair deepened her concern for the sufferings of the poor. Day converted to Catholicism followed the birth of her daughter. She became committed to a revolution of the heart, a revolution in which human individuals experience transforming change and the spiritual renewal that is the call of the Gospel to care for the hungry and despised.

In Peter Maurin, Day met a like-minded believer and reformer. In 1933, the two began the Catholic Worker Movement, which not only published an influential newspaper but founded a number of hospitality houses to serve the homeless.

After the United States entered World War II, Day wrote, "We are still pacifists. Our manifesto is the Sermon on the Mount, which means that we will try to be peacemakers. Speaking for many of our conscientious objectors, we will not participate in armed warfare or in making munitions, or by buying government bonds to prosecute the war, or in urging others to these efforts.

"But neither will we be carping in our criticism. We love our country, and we love our President. We have been the only country in the world where men of all nations have taken refuge from oppression. We recognize that while in the order of intention we have tried to stand for peace, for love of our brother, in the order of execution, we have failed as Americans in living up to our principles."

Day also wrote, "What we would like to do is change the world—make it a little simpler for people to feed, clothe, and shelter themselves as God intended them to do. And . . . by fighting for better conditions, by crying out unceasingly for the rights of the workers, of the poor, of the destitute . . . we can work for the oasis, the little cell of joy and peace in a harried world."

The author of these words has been considered for sainthood in the church she loved, but shortly before her death, in 1980, she said, "Don't call me a saint. I don't want to be dismissed so easily."

The biggest mistake, sometimes, is to play things
very safe in this life and end up being
moral failures.

Dorothy Day

Daniel Ellsberg

Political analyst, antinuclear activist; b. 1931, d. 2023

But I was not wrong . . . to hope that exposing secrets five presidents had withheld and the lies they told might have benefits for our democracy that were worthy of the risks. . . . Wouldn't you go to jail to help end the war?

Born in Chicago, Daniel Ellsworth graduated summa cum laude from Harvard in 1952 with a degree in economics. After three years in the U.S. Marine Corps, where he served as a rifle corps commander, he returned to Harvard to earn his Ph.D. in economics. From 1959 through 1971, the economist worked as a strategic analyst for the RAND Corporation; as a consultant for, and then special assistant in, the Department of Defense; and for the State Department at the U.S. embassy in Saigon. Beginning in 1969, while working again for the RAND Corporation, he privately photocopied a seven-thousand-page top secret study of America's intentions in Vietnam. Driven "by an urgent sense that [President] Nixon was about to escalate the war," Ellsberg gave the documents (known as the Pentagon Papers) to the Senate Foreign Relations Committee and, a year and a half later, to *The New York Times, The Washington Post,* and seventeen other newspapers. He explained that he did this in order "to reveal patterns of official deception."

After going underground for a brief period, Ellsberg was arrested and held for trial. The charges were dismissed, however, when it was learned that burglars working for the White House had broken into his psychiatrist's office, looking for evidence to use against him. *Secrets* (2002) is Ellsberg's "memoir of Vietnam and the Pentagon Papers." He also wrote a later memoir: *The Doomsday Machine: Confessions of a Nuclear War Planner* (2017).

Although best known for the Pentagon Papers, Ellsberg continued his commitment to exposing the government's war-related secrets until his death, in 2023. After the end of the Vietnam War, he said, "probably my main activity has been antinuclear lecturing, writing, and activism. I've been arrested between sixty to seventy times in that connection." In the early 1990s, Ellsberg worked for three years with Physicians for Social Responsibility, lobbying to end the nuclear arms race. In July 2004, he announced the Truth-Telling Project—his call for White House, Pentagon, and other federal employees to come forward and expose government lies and cover-ups—which, in turn, gave rise to the National Security Whistle-blowers Coalition. He also cofounded the Freedom of the Press Foundation and lent support to many individual whistle-blowers who came after him, including Sibel Edmonds, Chelsea Manning, Edward Snowden, and Julian Assange. Honored with numerous awards, Ellsberg received the 2018 Olof Palme Prize for his "profound humanism and exceptional moral courage" and, in 2022, the Sam Adams Award.

Accused by some of treason, he responded, "We live in a country, thank God, where telling the truth to Congress is not treason." A person who sees what Ellsberg did as treason, he says, "in my judgment does not understand the founding principles of this country very well."

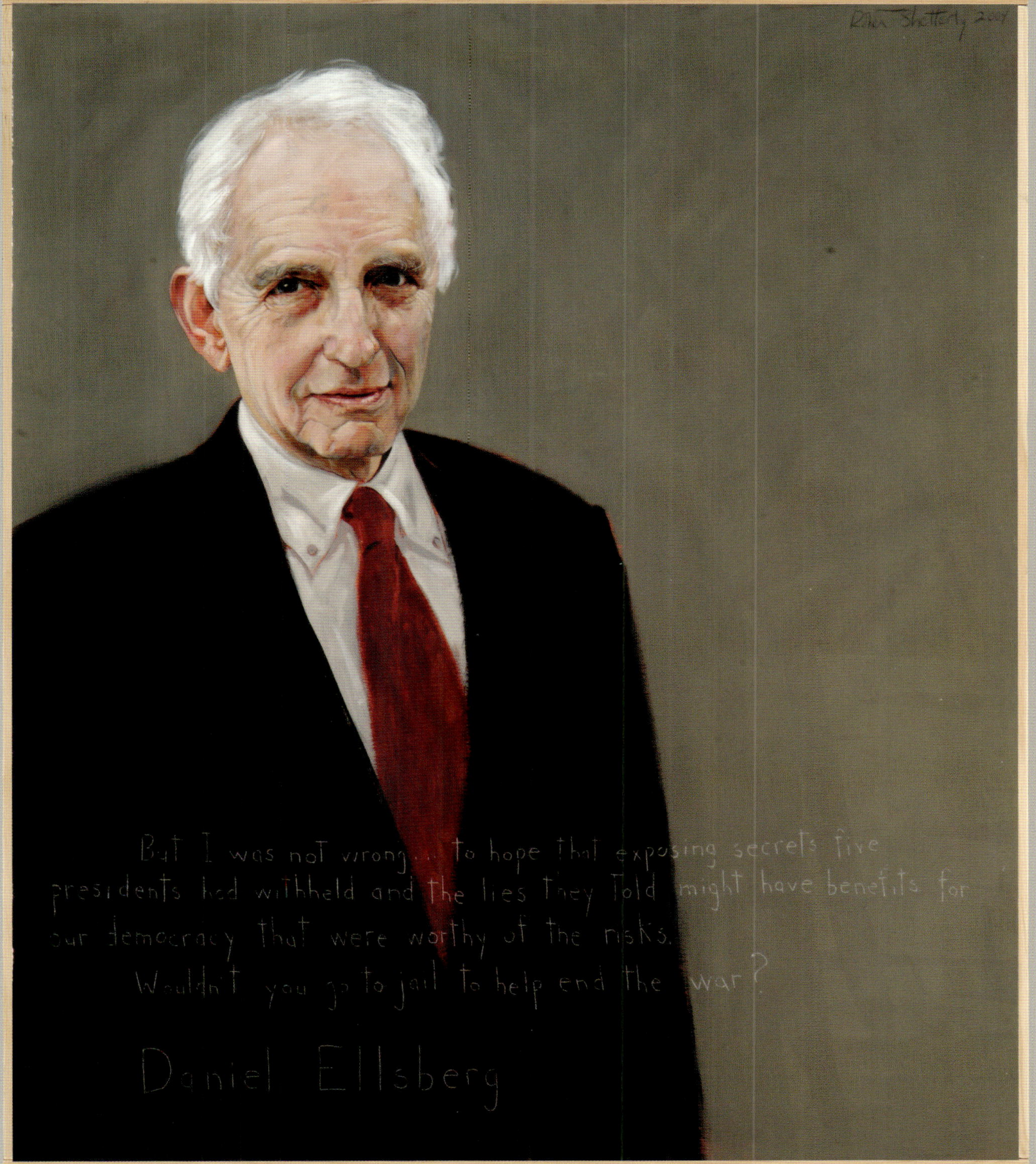
But I was not wrong... to hope that exposing secrets five presidents had withheld and the lies they told might have benefits for our democracy that were worthy of the risks.
Wouldn't you go to jail to help end the war?
Daniel Ellsberg

Bruce Gagnon

Veteran, organizer; b. 1952

The role of the U.S. in the new world corporate order is going to be to export security. That means endless wars and weapons in space. The Pentagon will send our kids off to foreign lands to suppress opposition to corporate globalization. How will we ever end America's addiction to war and violence as long as our communities are dependent on military spending for jobs? We must work to convert the military-industrial complex to sustainable technologies like windpower, solar, and mass transit.

When Bruce Gagnon was vice president of the Okaloosa County (Florida) Young Republican Club, he volunteered in Richard Nixon's 1968 presidential campaign. Today, as cofounder and secretary/coordinator of the Global Network Against Weapons and Nuclear Power in Space (GN), he fights the reach of corporate greed into space, which pits him against most Washington officials.

Getting his start as a state coordinator of the Florida Coalition for Peace & Justice, Gagnon has worked on space issues for more than forty years. Valuable resources on the moon and planets form the next battleground for corporate profit, he says, and "defense" programs such as Star Wars actually are conceived as offense. "The U.S. intends to control . . . and dominate space and deny other countries access," says Gagnon, adding that the high-tech military programs used to seize this control threaten everyone on Earth and divert funding from the common good.

Gagnon speaks internationally on this high-stakes topic and has written for publications such as *Earth Island Journal, CounterPunch, Z Magazine,* *Space News, National Catholic Reporter, Asia Times, Le Monde diplomatique,* and *Canadian Dimension.* He has produced two videos, *Arsenal of Hypocrisy* (2003) and *Battle for America's Soul* (2005) and has published a book, *Come Together Right Now: Organizing Stories from a Fading Empire* (2005). From 2003 to 2020, Gagnon hosted *This Issue,* a cable TV program that aired on seventeen stations in Maine, his home state. He also writes a blog, *Organizing Notes,* for Global Network.

Gagnon's work has not yet drawn the attention it warrants. Television's *60 Minutes* tuned in to his Cancel Cassini Campaign against the 1997 launch of plutonium into space. But Project Censored, based at Sonoma State University in California, found articles by Gagnon to be among the most censored stories of 1999 and 2005.

Remembering that his own shift in consciousness began with a handful of Vietnam War protestors who stood outside an air force base in California where he was stationed, Bruce Gagnon perseveres—and finds new ways to enlist the concern of others.

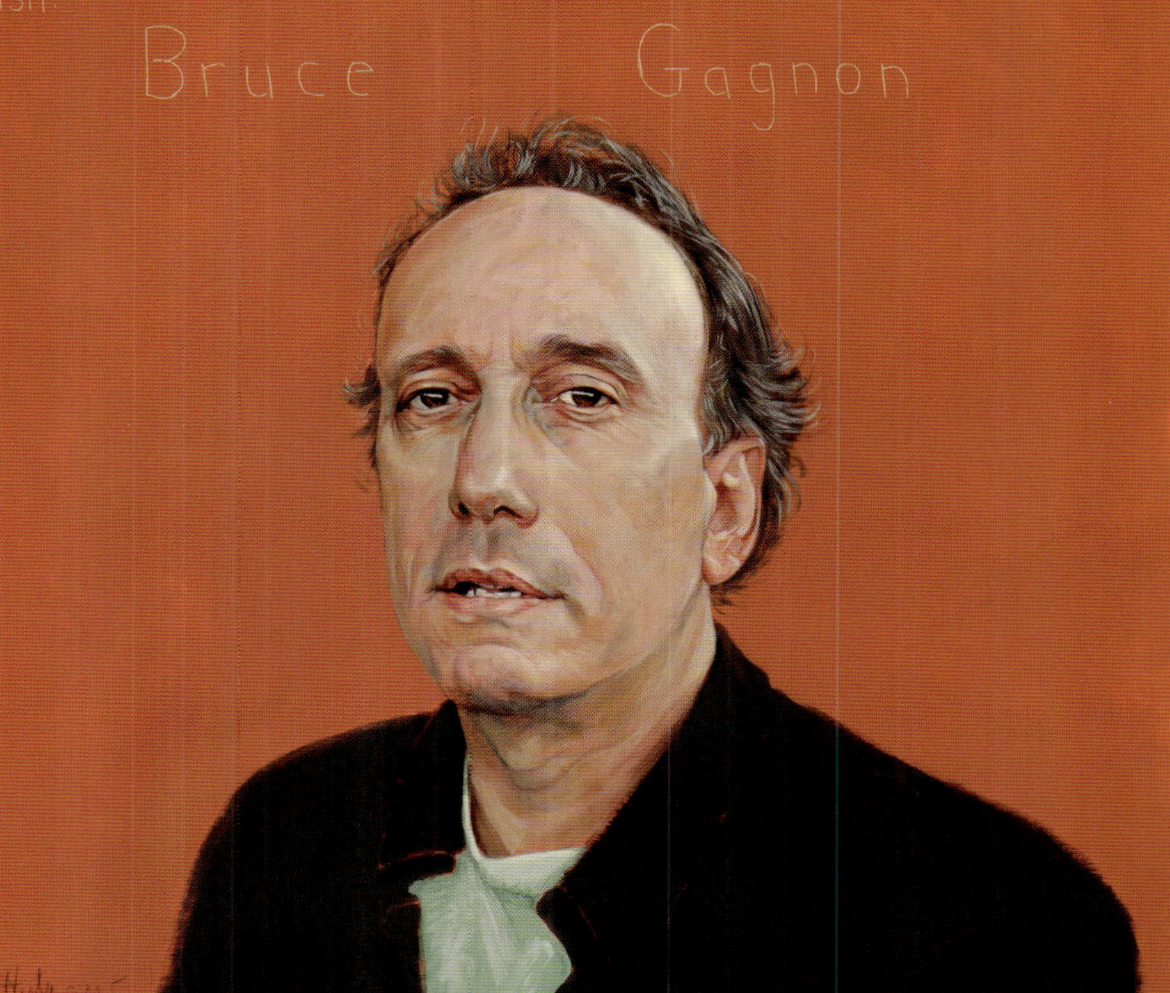

The role of the U.S. in the new world corporate order is going to be to export security. That means endless wars and weapons in space. The Pentagon will send our kids off to foreign lands to suppress opposition to corporate globalization. How will we ever end America's addiction to war and violence as long as our communities are dependent on military spending for jobs? We must work to convert the military industrial complex to sustainable technologies like windpower, solar and mass transit.

Bruce   Gagnon

Emma Goldman

Anarchist, feminist, labor advocate; b. 1869, d. 1940

. . . the greatest bulwark of capitalism is militarism.

Emma Goldman was born in Kovno, Russia, and emigrated to live with a sister in Rochester, New York, when she was sixteen. Her family's financial hardships forced her to leave school and become a laborer; her first job in America was as a seamstress in a clothing factory.

Goldman's political consciousness was shaped by reading (Chernyshevsky, Kropotkin), by her first-hand knowledge of miserable working conditions, and, most dramatically, by the violent outcome of the 1886 demonstrations on behalf of the eight-hour workday at Haymarket Square in Chicago; despite an absence of proof, seven anarchists were executed for allegedly causing the deaths of seven policemen. In 1889, Goldman moved to New York, where she became a protégée of Johann Most, the editor of an anarchist paper. From 1906 until 1917, she and her partner, Alexander Berkman, edited and published their own paper, *Mother Earth*. She wrote five books: *Anarchism and Other Essays* (1910), *Social Significance of the Modern Drama* (1914), *My Disillusionment in Russia* (1923), *My Further Disillusionment in Russia* (1924), and *Living My Life* (1931).

In her writing and public speaking, Goldman was a gadfly. She championed free speech, birth control, women's equality, and labor unions. She said, "The history of progress is written in the blood of men and women who have dared to espouse an unpopular cause, as, for instance, the black man's right to his body, or woman's right to her soul." Today many may take these rights for granted, but a century ago her words challenged the national conscience. Another of her bold statements still resonates today: ". . . if the production of any commodity necessitates the sacrifice of human life, society should do without that commodity, but it can not do without that life."

Goldman was arrested and detained several times for her activism, but her most severe punishment—two years in prison—was for obstructing the draft during World War I.

In 1919, she and Berkman were deported to Russia, where she witnessed the aftermath of the 1917 Revolution. At odds with the Bolshevik dictatorship, she left in 1921. She was permitted to reenter the United States on a speaking tour in 1934. Marriage to a Scottish anarchist working in Wales gained her English citizenship, and she lived in London during the Spanish Civil War (1936–1939). Goldman visited Spain several times during the conflict, where she sought refuge for women and children displaced by the war and spoke out against the forces of fascism.

Emma Goldman died in Toronto in 1940 and is buried in Forest Park, Illinois, a few miles from Haymarket Square.

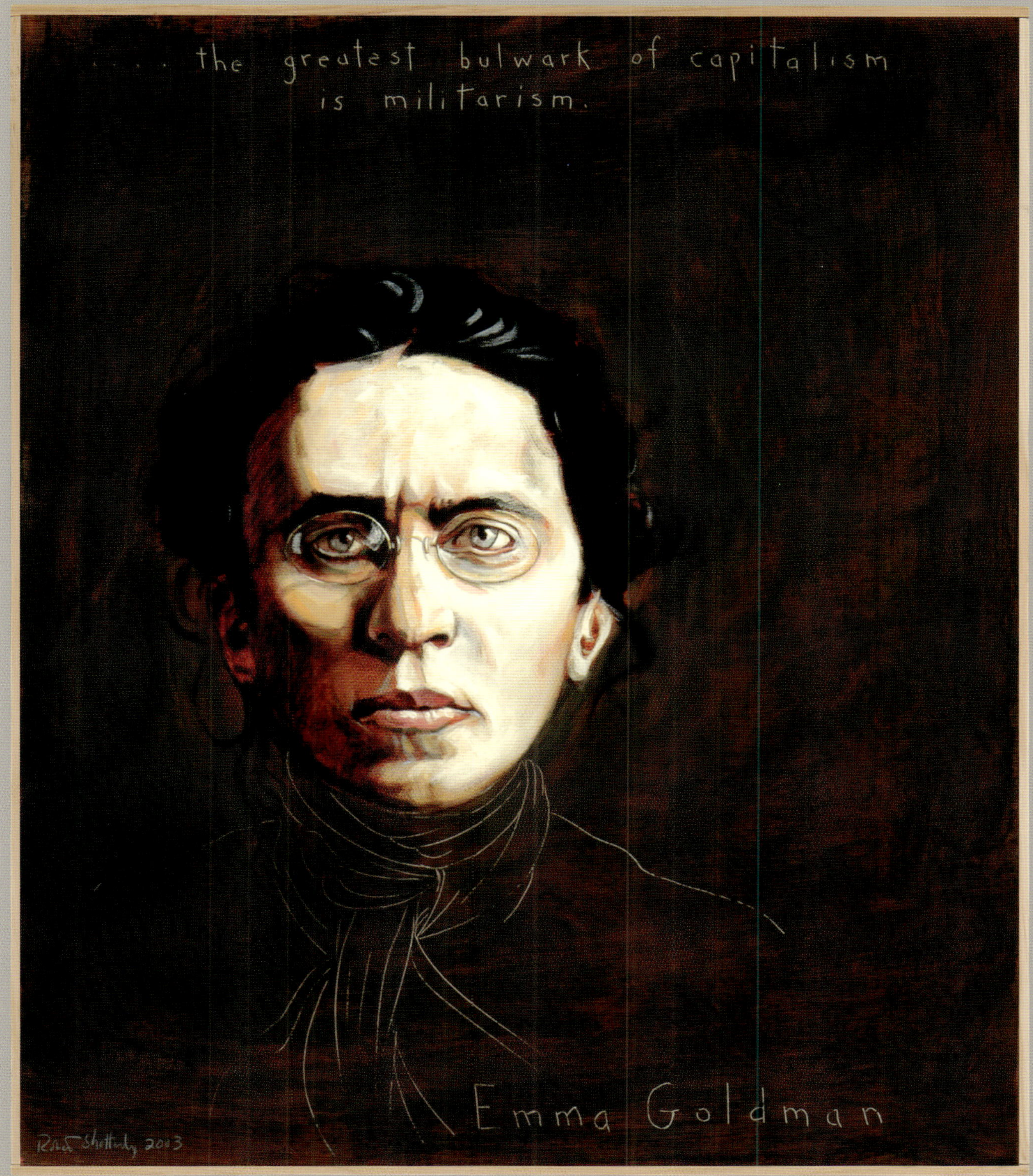
..... the greatest bulwark of capitalism
is militarism.
Emma Goldman

Amy Goodman

Journalist, host of *Democracy Now!***; b. 1957**

I really do think that if for one week in the United States we saw the true face of war, we saw people's limbs sheared off, we saw kids blown apart, for one week, war would be eradicated. Instead, what we see in the U.S. media . . . is the video war game. . . . Our mission is to make dissent commonplace in America.

When asked what she represents, Amy Goodman has the perfect answer: "Democracy Now." As host of the only national radio/TV news show free of all corporate underwriting, she can present a range of independent voices not often heard on the airwaves. "Dissent is what makes this country healthy," she explains.

Goodman grew up on Long Island, the descendant of Hasidic rabbis and the daughter of radical parents. After graduating from Harvard in 1984 with a degree in anthropology, she spent ten years as producer of the evening news show at WBAI, Pacifica Radio's station in New York City. *Democracy Now!*, which she cofounded in 1996, airs on more than fourteen hundred stations worldwide.

The title of the 2004 book Goodman wrote with her brother David, *The Exception to the Rulers*, clearly defines her expectation for media. "The role of reporters," she says, "is to go to where the silence is and say something." For going to places like East Timor, Nigeria, Peru, and Haiti to report on stories ignored by the mainstream media—often at considerable risk—she has won many honors, including the Gandhi Peace Award for her "significant contribution to the promotion of an enduring international peace" and the I. F. Stone Medal for Journalistic Independence by Harvard University's Nieman Foundation. She has been arrested several times while trying to report the news, including at the 2008 Republican National Convention in St. Paul, Minnesota, and during the 2016 Dakota Access Pipeline protest in Morton County, North Dakota. Her most recent book, *Democracy Now! Twenty Years Covering the Movements Changing America* (2016; coauthored with David Goodman and Denis Moynihan), highlights her critical role as a high-profile independent journalist.

"She begins broadcasting at 7 a.m., and works until near midnight," a reporter wrote in *The Washington Post*. Her fellow journalist Danny Schechter has said about her, "She works hard and when she's not working, she works harder. She is earnest to a fault, with little patience for folks who may have a more nuanced stance on certain issues than she does. But she is informed, committed, passionate, thorough and very uncompromising." Goodman is, Schechter says, "in a class of her own."

I really do think that if for one week in the United States we saw the true face of war, we saw people's limbs sheared off, we saw kids blown apart, for one week, war would be eradicated. Instead, what we see. in the U.S. media. . . is the video war game. . . . Our mission is to make dissent commonplace in America.

Amy
Goodman

Doris "Granny D" Haddock

Activist; b. 1910, d. 2010

Just as an unbalanced mind can accumulate mental stresses that can grow and take on a life of their own, so little decisions of our modern life can accumulate to the point where our society finds itself bombing other people for their oil, or supporting dictators who torture whole populations—all so that our unbalanced interests might be served.

Born Ethel Doris Rollins in Laconia, New Hampshire, "Granny D" is best known today for her 1999–2000 walk across America in support of campaign finance reform. Her trip, begun shortly before her eighty-ninth birthday, lasted fourteen months and covered 3,200 miles.

Haddock's journey was no mere publicity stunt. She had studied the issue of campaign finance reform so that she could communicate her views to the people who assembled to meet her along the way, including the more than two thousand who greeted her arrival in Washington, D.C. She spent a year training for the physical challenges she would encounter on the trip, which would wear out four pairs of shoes and include a hundred-mile stretch that she covered on cross-country skis.

Commitment to campaign finance reform is but one facet of an activist career that included working on environmental issues in Alaska (1960) and writing and speaking against war in Iraq (2003). She told her fellow citizens, "We must not be content to go home and watch television when there is a democracy to run, or to spend all our money on ourselves and our children. Right now, many young people will tell you to 'get a life' if you suggest that they get involved in community issues. But that is a life. That is the life of free people in a democracy."

Haddock's nickname reflects her status as great-grandmother of a large family; it also helps to define the strong, protective love she felt for her country. "We live in a land where each person's voice matters. We can all do something. Sometimes, we have to make sacrifices to be heard. But it is still our free land and, my, how we all do love it," she said.

In her moral toughness and pragmatism, "Granny D" also knew that real love acts responsibly and fights for its object: "We have a duty to look after each other. If we lose control of our government, then we lose our ability to dispense justice and human kindness. Our first priority today, then, is to defeat utterly those forces of greed and corruption that have come between us and our self-governance."

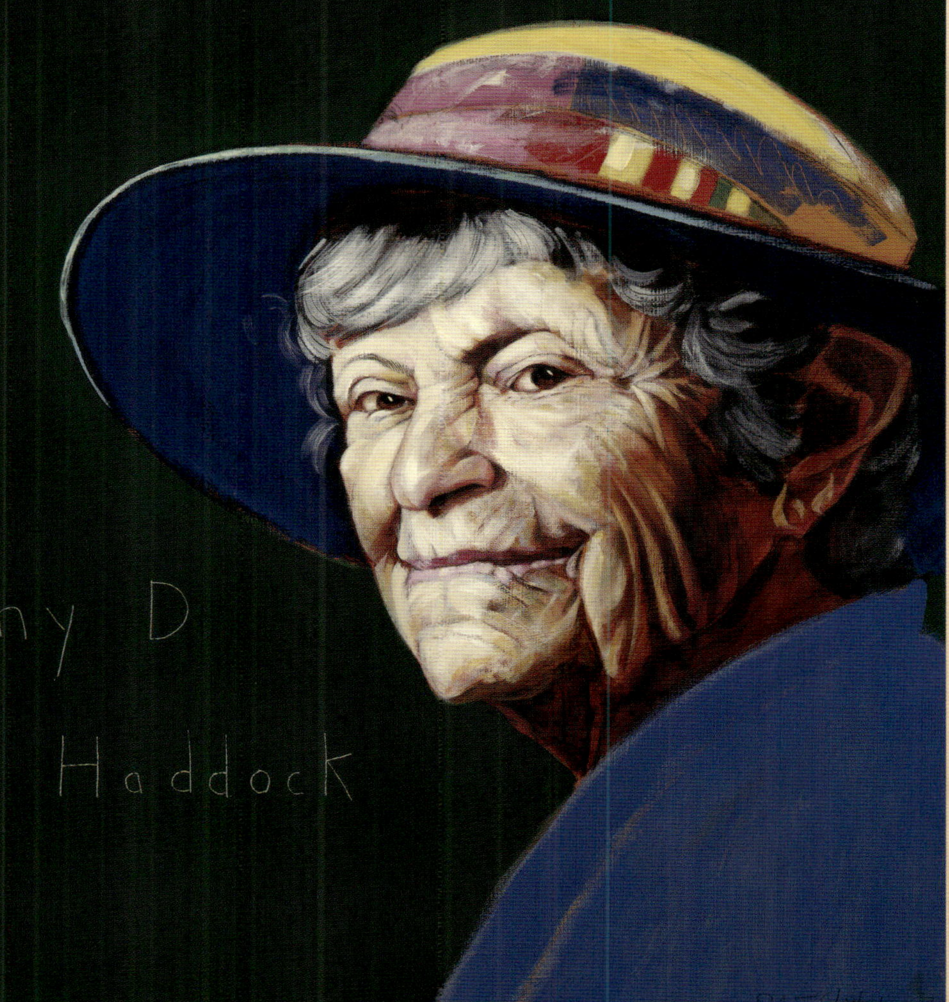

Just as an unbalanced mind can accumulate mental stresses that can grow and take on a life of their own, so the little decisions of our modern life can accumulate to the point where our society finds itself bombing other people for their oil, or supporting dictators who torture whole populations — all so that our unbalanced interests might be served.

Granny D

Doris Haddock

Daniel Hale

Intelligence analyst; whistle-blower; b. 1987

With drone warfare, sometimes nine out of ten people killed are innocent. You have to kill part of your conscience to do your job. But what possibly could I have done to cope with the undeniable cruelties that I perpetuated? The thing I feared most was the temptation not to question it. So I contacted an investigative reporter . . . and told him I had something the American people needed to know.

Before sentencing, Daniel Hale began his eleven-page letter to Judge Liam O'Grady with a quotation from U.S. Navy Admiral Gene LaRocque: "We now kill people without ever seeing them. Now you push a button thousands of miles away . . . since it's all done by remote control, there's no remorse . . . and then we come home in triumph."

Daniel Hale is a former intelligence contractor who disclosed to *The Intercept* information pertaining to the American drone warfare program. Hale was driven by a sense of guilt over his role in identifying targets for drone strikes. He was first charged in 2019 with multiple counts, including theft of government property and disclosing intelligence information. In March 2021, Hale pleaded guilty to violating the Espionage Act and in July was sentenced to forty-five months in prison.

Hale grew up in a rural mountain community in Tennessee. Though critical of the armed forces, he joined the air force after suffering from homelessness and believing that he had few other options. Hale was assigned to the National Security Agency as an intelligence analyst from 2009 to 2013. He worked for the Joint Special Operations Task Force at Bagram Air Base in Afghanistan, where, as a signals analyst, he was tasked with "identifying, tracking, and targeting" terror suspects for assassination. Hale was troubled by "the uncertainty if anyone I was involved in killing or capturing was a civilian or not. There's no way of knowing." Throughout his service, as he witnessed children inadvertently killed in air strikes, Hale became more convinced that the war had "little

to do with preventing terror from coming into the United States and a lot more to do with protecting the profits of weapons manufacturers and so-called defense contractors."

Hale experienced post-traumatic stress and depression following his deployment with the air force to Afghanistan in 2012. He left the air force, became a contractor at the National Geospatial-Intelligence Agency, and began to speak out against U.S. drone policy, the U.S. targeted killing program, and U.S. foreign policy.

The documents Hale leaked to Jeremy Scahill of *The Intercept* in 2013 exposed that, from January 2012 to February 2013, U.S. special operations air strikes killed over two hundred people, only thirty-five of whom were the intended targets. During one period of five months, close to 90 percent of the victims killed were not intended targets. The documents further disclosed how the government chose its targets. Hale's leaks have called attention to the U.S. military practice of categorizing people killed in drone strikes as "enemies killed in action" unless proven contrary, possibly underrepresenting the estimates of civilian deaths. Hale played a prominent role in the 2016 documentary *National Bird*, which follows the stories of three whistle-blowers determined to end the silence surrounding the United States' use of drone attacks.

In 2021, Hale received the Sam Adams Award for Integrity in Intelligence from a group of whistle-blowers within the national security community as well as the International Whistleblowing Award from the Australian organization Blueprint for Free Speech.

With drone warfare, sometimes nine out of ten people killed are innocent. You have to kill part of your conscience to do your job... But what possibly could I have done to cope with the undeniable cruelties that I perpetuated? The thing I feared most...was the temptation not to question it. So I contacted an investigative reporter...and told him I had something the American people needed to know.

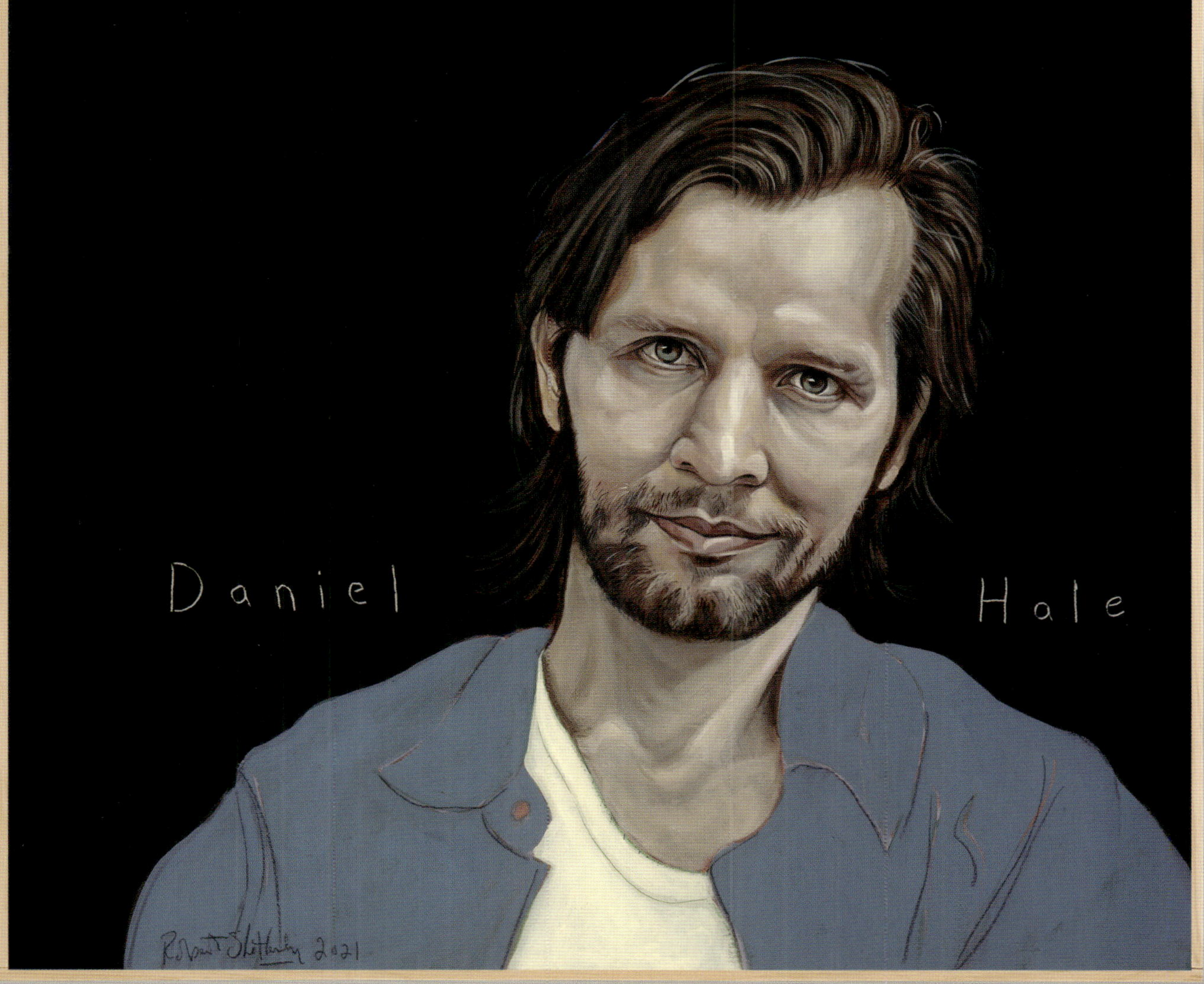

Jim Harney

Photojournalist, advocate for the undocumented; b. 1940, d. 2008

I could hear five-hundred-pound bombs going off, and see A-37 jets that my country had sent down to El Salvador, and we were in a dirt-floor hut and those who could read shared some Scripture . . . and one of them a mother breast feeding her baby, and the A-37 jets came in. . . . And then the woman brought me out of the hut, and as the bombs were going off in the valley she pointed to the planes coming in and she said they come from a part of the world where people believe in a God of death. We believe in a God of the living, and when you believe in the God of the living, she said you end up doing things that you never dreamt yourself capable of doing.

The Merriam-Webster dictionary defines the word *globalization* as "the development of an increasingly integrated global economy marked especially by free trade, free flow of capital, and the tapping of cheaper foreign labor markets." The dictionary does not define the consequences for people who are squeezed out of this more modern economy. Jim Harney called those people the undocumented, or the excluded. For decades, Harney's work was to bring a voice, a face, and a story to these undocumented people.

Jim Harney grew up in a Catholic "ghetto" in the greater Boston area, where Catholic communities, complete with their own schools, hospitals, and churches, existed in isolation from the non-Catholic neighborhoods around them. Harney became a priest in the sixties, and during that decade two major events came to inform his worldview. The first was the directive from the Second Vatican Council to open Catholicism to the world, in essence opening Harney and the "ghettos" to interaction and dialogues with their neighbors in the non-Catholic communities. The second event was the Vietnam War, which set Harney onto the activist path he'd follow for the rest of his life.

In 1968, Harney and thirteen other antiwar activists broke into some draft board offices, stole files, and burned them with homemade napalm. Known as the Milwaukee 14, they all went to prison for more than a year. Spending much of his time in solitary confinement with only the Bible to read, Harney was released with a new purpose: to follow and spend time with the world's poor and degraded people.

Armed with a camera, Harney went anyplace and everyplace where there was suffering—Haiti, Argentina, Venezuela, and beyond. He returned with photographs and stories of the struggles of the poor. He amassed thousands of photos, which he turned into slide-show presentations. He studied finance to better understand and explain how globalization affects the poor. "U.S. citizens in particular bear a responsibility to hear the testimony of the Madres-Mothers of those 'disappeared' by the U.S. School of the Americas (SOA) graduates and to understand that someone else pays the difference for our 'bargains' at the mall."

In the 1990s, Harney moved to Bangor, Maine, and became an artist in residence for Posibilidad, a group of activists formed in 1999 that "engages people in conversation around the excluded of society."

In 2008, after being diagnosed with terminal cancer, Harney planned his own long walk from Boston to Washington, D.C., to raise awareness of immigration issues and to talk with anyone along the way who would listen. He made it as far as Providence, Rhode Island.

Harney's legacy lives on in his images, stories, and words. Harney said, "I go on the premise that when people who are not suffering see the pain on this planet, they change."

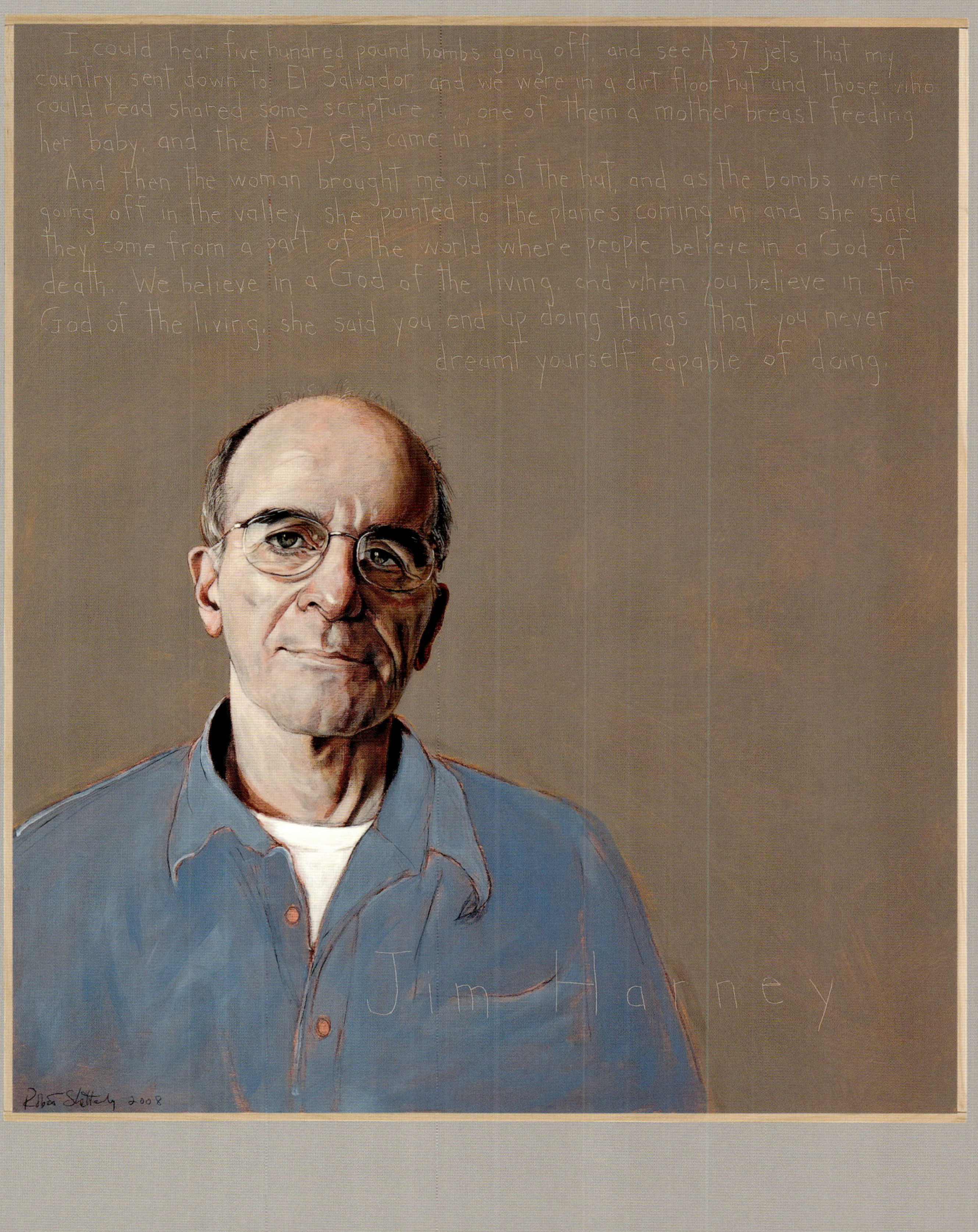

I could hear five hundred pound bombs going off, and see A-37 jets that my country sent down to El Salvador and we were in a dirt floor hut and those who could read shared some scripture . . . one of them a mother breast feeding her baby, and the A-37 jets came in . . .
And then the woman brought me out of the hut, and as the bombs were going off in the valley, she pointed to the planes coming in and she said they come from a part of the world where people believe in a God of death. We believe in a God of the living, and when you believe in the God of the living, she said you end up doing things that you never dreamt yourself capable of doing.
Jim Harney
Robert Shetterly 2008

Chris Hedges

War correspondent, writer; b. 1956

Once we sign on for war's crusade, once we see ourselves on the side of the angels, once we embrace a theological or ideological belief system that defines itself as the embodiment of goodness and light, it is only a matter of how we will carry out murder.

Chris Hedges, the son of a Presbyterian minister, was born on September 18, 1956, in St. Johnsbury, Vermont. He graduated from Colgate University with a B.A. in English literature and went on to receive a master of divinity degree from Harvard. He has an honorary doctorate from Starr King School for the Ministry in Berkeley, California, and in 2014 was ordained as a Presbyterian minister.

Hedges spent nearly two decades as a foreign correspondent in Central America, the Middle East, Africa, and the Balkans. He was an early and outspoken critic of the U.S. plan to invade and occupy Iraq and called the press coverage at the time "shameful cheerleading." In 2002, he was a member of *The New York Times* reporting team that won a Pulitzer Prize for its coverage of global terrorism. That same year he won an Amnesty International Global Award for Human Rights Journalism.

In 2003, shortly after the war in Iraq began, during a commencement speech at Rockford College, Hedges told the graduating class, ". . . we are embarking on an occupation that, if history is any guide, will be as damaging to our souls as it will be to our prestige, power, and security." His speech caused an uproar; Hedges was escorted off campus by security officials before the diplomas were awarded. This event made national news. *The Wall Street Journal* ran an editorial denouncing his antiwar stance, and *The New York Times* issued a formal reprimand, forbidding Hedges to speak about the war. Hedges resigned shortly thereafter and became a senior fellow at the Nation Institute.

A prolific writer, Hedges is the author of sixteen books, beginning with the 2002 bestseller *War Is a Force That Gives Us Meaning,* an examination of what war does to individuals and societies. He states that war is the pornography of violence, a powerful narcotic that "has a dark beauty, filled with the monstrous and the grotesque." Of his own experience of war, living and working as a journalist in the war zones of Central America, the Balkans, and the Middle East, he writes, "I have seen too much of violent death. I have tasted too much of my own fear. I have painful memories that lie buried and untouched most of the time. It is never easy when they surface." For his book, *Collateral Damage* (2008), Hedges interviewed combat veterans who had testified on the record about atrocities carried out by American soldiers and marines during the military occupation of Iraq. Most recently, he published *The Greatest Evil Is War* (2022).

In order to maintain his independence as a journalist, Hedges now publishes a weekly column and weekly podcast, *The Chris Hedges Report,* on Substack.

Once we sign on for war's crusade, once we see ourselves on the side of the
angels, once we embrace a theological or ideological belief system that defines
itself as the embodiment of goodness and light, it is only a matter of how
we will carry out murder.

Chris
Hedges

Pat Humphries

Singer/songwriter; b. 1960

Came home from school to the war on TV / Looked at the soldiers and thought I saw me. / Looked at the children and saw my own face. / I saw myself dying all over the place.

Think of calls for social justice, sung loudly rather than shouted. Songs to embrace, sing along with, and even dance to. Songs to inspire courage, build community, and create peace. Songs by Pete Seeger, Woody Guthrie, and Pat Humphries—one half, along with Sandy O, of the activist duo Emma's Revolution. This is Pat's tale.

Pat Humphries was born in Ohio in 1960, not far from Kent State University. She started singing and playing guitar as a young child. In 1970, at an anti–Vietnam War demonstration at Kent State, where some of her sisters were attending school, the Ohio National Guard shot and killed four peaceful student demonstrators. It affected Humphries and her family personally and, at the young age of ten, triggered her dedication to activism.

As a teenager, Humphries traveled and performed with youth choruses and began playing in Cleveland coffeehouses, learning folk music. As Humphries puts it, "The subject matter that I was singing about had been amply covered by other singers and I wanted to sing about something else. I left school, got a day job organizing arts events and started writing songs. . . . I was affected by the feminist movement, the anti-nuclear movement, the farmworker boycotts, the lesbian and gay movement, the American Indian movement and the environmental movement."

"Never Turning Back," which she composed at a songwriting workshop, became an unofficial theme song of the United Nations Fourth Conference on Women in Beijing in 1995. Pete Seeger called it "one of the best songs I've heard in 50 years."

Humphries has written social justice songs for women, migrant workers, and anyone whose voices and stories need to be heard. She has traveled across the United States and to Cuba and Nicaragua. When NPR played Humphries's song "Swimming to the Other Side" on its program *All Things Considered* in 2002, her name moved into the national spotlight.

By this time, she had met Sandy Opatow (O), and they had formed a duo. While trying to work out a name for their group, they hit upon Emma Goldman's popular quote, "If I can't dance, I don't want to be part of your revolution"; they became Emma's Revolution.

After the 9/11 attacks, Humphries and Sandy O composed "Peace Salaam Shalom" (peace in English, Arabic, and Hebrew), and they played it loudly in protest of the Iraq war. Humphries said, "Clearly work had to be done in the wake of the bombing. There was a need of mutual understanding of what peace means—that's at the heart of the work that we do." Humphries's song "We Are One" was chosen as the theme for a 2003 conference in Washington, D.C., on the reunification of North and South Korea. Emma's Revolution went to Korea with the conference organizers, and they had the song translated into Korean so they could perform it in both languages. In 2009, Emma's Revolution played at the first-ever Peace Ball for President Barack Obama's inauguration.

Pat Humphries believes in music as a powerful force in the struggle for justice and, with a busy 2024 concert schedule, is still singing her heart out.

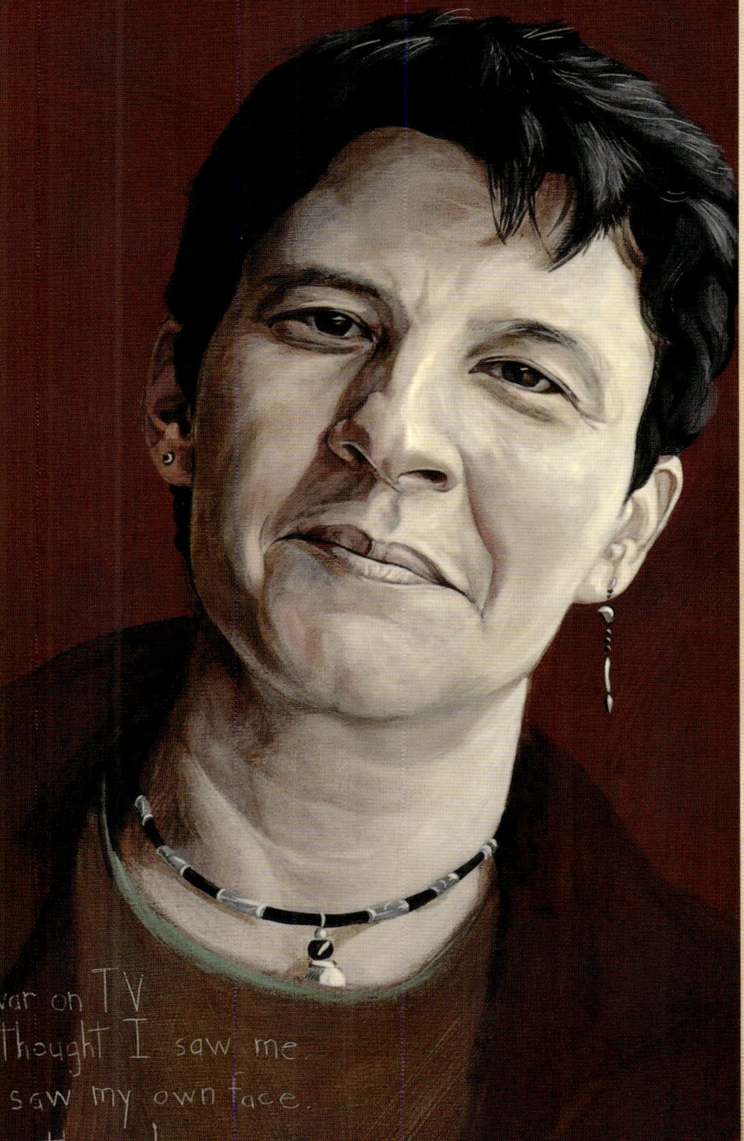

Pat Humphries

Came home from school to the war on TV
Looked at the soldiers and thought I saw me.
Looked at the children and saw my own face.
I saw myself dying all over the place.

John Hunter

Educator, musician, World Peace Game inventor; b. 1954

Find out what a child's passion is, what she really cares about, and build the curriculum to that, build it around her desire, her passion, so that she will feel not only that you respect her deepest feeling, but care enough to respond in a way that makes her feel valued. Suddenly, the learning seems more enjoyable, more accessible, more attractive to the child. It involves something, some aspect of what she cares about.

Education visionary and fourth-grade public school teacher John Hunter is optimistic about the fate of the world, despite its seemingly intractable problems. His positive attitude comes from decades of watching nine- and ten-year-olds solve the toughest global problems he can throw at them in an open-ended political science simulation he calls the World Peace Game.

Hunter first created the game in 1978 at an urban high school in Richmond, Virginia, where he had landed his first teaching job. The game evolved over time into an elaborate four-tiered Plexiglass structure that dominated the center of his classroom at Agnor-Hurt Elementary School in Charlottesville, Virginia.

The game is deliberately designed so students "fail massively at first, but we create a safe environment, with great care and love, where it's okay to fail and learn from that," he says. The thirty-player, fifty-problem nature of the World Peace Game is so complex, "it immediately plunges students into uncertainty," and as play progresses, "the rules and situations change, with multiple consequences, most of them hidden," says its inventor.

At first glance, it looks like a competition between different teams, but "about halfway through, they have a sudden realization that they are on the same side. Everything is interrelated. To win, they have to go into a hyper-collaborative state." In order for anyone to win, says Hunter, "everyone has to win." Not only do they negotiate peace, but each country must wind up with an improved economy, as well.

Hunter's encouragement of problem solving, cooperation, and higher-order thinking has earned recognition and awards for him and his students. They're the subjects of a documentary film and of Hunter's celebrated 2011 TED Talk. Hunter's book *World Peace and Other Fourth Grade Achievements* (2013) also tells the story of the game's development and success with students. In 2012, Hunter and his students were invited to explain their strategies to U.S. Secretary of Defense Leon Panetta and his staff at the Pentagon.

Hunter has set up the World Peace Game Foundation to train facilitators around the world, bringing his award-winning curriculum to schools everywhere. "The WPG is not a permanent system, but rather a temporary, internalized, flexible and renewable practice," says Hunter.

Despite its wild success and growth, the game's fundamental principles remain: Allow students the luxury of failure, encourage them not to be afraid of complexity, and help them develop empathy and compassion. "The World Peace Game," Hunter says, "is about learning to live and work comfortably in the unknown."

Outside the classroom, music is an important part of Hunter's life; he has been both a studio musician and a live performer with the Ululating Mummies, an avant-garde world music band based in Richmond, Virginia.

Find out what a child's passion is, what she really cares
about, and build the curriculum to that, build it around
her desire, her passion, so that she will feel not only that
you respect her deepest feeling, but care enough about
her to respond in a way that makes her feel valued.
Suddenly, the learning seems more enjoyable, more
accessible, more attractive to the child. It involves something,
some aspect of what she cares about.

John Hunter

Dahr Jamail

Independent journalist, war reporter; b. 1968

It was a failure of citizenship by the American people that the Bush cabal was allowed to invade Iraq. Thus, every U.S. citizen who is not doing everything in their power to end this illegal and immoral occupation as quickly as possible is complicit with the war crimes being committed in Iraq on a daily basis.

In early 2003, Dahr Jamail was working as a guide at Denali, the highest mountain in North America, writing about climbing for an independent Alaskan newspaper, and saving up his money. Then the drumbeat for war in Iraq destroyed his peace. As he read foreign and independent news and "did the usual stuff to express dissent," he was infuriated by what he saw as the corporate media's cooperation with the Bush administration.

When the Iraq invasion began, Jamail, a fourth-generation Lebanese American who grew up in Houston, decided he could sit at home, depressed and angry, or he could take action. He bought a laptop computer, a digital camera, and a plane ticket.

Between November 2003 and February 2005, Jamail spent eight months in Iraq, reporting on the war's "collateral damage" in much greater detail than the journalists embedded with the military acknowledged. He wrote of soldiers shooting people who were praying at a Baghdad mosque. He relayed accounts of civilians in Fallujah with extraordinary, unexplained burns (later revealed to be caused by white phosphorus) and of men and women who were shot as they tried to swim to safety across the Euphrates River while carrying white surrender flags. Jamail also documented who was profiting from the war, reporting the blurring of the lines between the military and corporations operating in Iraq. One such example was Bechtel's failure to restore potable water to Iraqis after being paid hundreds of millions to do so.

Acknowledging his reliance on Iraqi interpreters, Jamail said, "I trust them. They put their lives on the line to even be seen with me, in an effort to get the truth out."

After starting with a homemade press pass and no outlet but email, Jamail created a website and began writing for the Inter Press Service, *The Asia Times*, and *The Nation*, among others. Also, he has reported for *Democracy Now!* and the BBC. At the culminating session of the World Tribunal on Iraq in June 2005, he documented U.S. violations of Fourth Geneva Convention provisions for health care in occupied countries. By the fall of 2005, Jamail's interpreters said it was too dangerous for them to help him inside Iraq. His articles and email dispatches continued as he gathered information by phone and email and from Arab and other foreign media. He toured the United States as a speaker. "It's not about defense," he says. "It's about money, and that, to me, is the greatest travesty of all."

Jamail's book about what he learned in Iraq, *Beyond the Green Zone: Dispatches from an Unembedded Journalist in Occupied Iraq,* was published in 2007. He wrote a follow-up about active dissent within the military, *The Will to Resist: Soldiers Who Refuse to Fight in Iraq and Afghanistan* (2009).

Since the end of those wars, Jamail has continued his work as a journalist, earning many awards and writing two more books. Most recently, his reporting has focused on the climate crisis.

Says Jamail, "Since an informed citizenry is the basis for a healthy democracy, independent, noncorporate media are more crucial today than ever before."

It was a failure of citizenship by the American people that the Bush cabal was allowed to invade Iraq. Thus, any US citizen who is not doing everything in their power to end this illegal and immoral occupation as quickly as possible is complicit with the war crimes being committed in Iraq on a daily basis.

Dahr Jamail

Joyce and Nelson Johnson

Civil rights activists; Nelson b. 1943; Joyce b. 1946

No nation can endure that violates truth. One human truth is that we are all called to honor the dignity, worth, and potential of each person, as well as the Earth itself. The failure to do so causes on-going conflict and violence and ultimately lays the foundation for civil war, but there is hope as we learn to speak truth and walk together.

Nelson Johnson and Joyce Hobson met during the winter of 1969, when the two were already activists. A graduate of Duke University—one of six Black students admitted to her class—Joyce had helped found the school's Afro-American Society and organized protests for more inclusive education at Duke. Nelson had attended the predominantly Black North Carolina A&T State University, led protest marches, supported striking university cafeteria workers, and founded the Greensboro Association of Poor People. When they met and fell in love, the two talked of working together to end racism before returning to more traditional professional careers.

Tensions in Greensboro were rising during the spring of 1969, when the school system refused to seat the winner of the Black Dudley High School election for student council president. When the police began beating up striking students, Greensboro's Black community and the students at A&T became agitated; armed skirmishes between police and citizens escalated. Then Greensboro's mayor ordered the National Guard onto the A&T campus, where they overwhelmed the dorms with tear gas, helicopters, and 650 troops. The next day, as tanks rolled by the A&T campus, Nelson and Joyce were married.

Over the following years, the Johnsons organized laborers, inadequately housed tenants, and students around the country. While working to organize and unify white and Black textile-mill workers in Greensboro in 1979, they planned an anti-Klan march and conference. The morning of the event a caravan of nine cars carrying Klansmen and American Nazis arrived at the start of the march. A fight broke out. Then shooting erupted, killing five of the labor activists and injuring many more. Although Nelson Johnson had obtained a parade permit and the assurance that the police would protect the march, there were no police present when the white supremacists arrived that morning at Morningside Homes, a Black public housing development. Despite video of the shooting, all-white juries acquitted the Klan and Nazi shooters, after both state and federal criminal trials. Later, a federal civil trial found Klansmen, Nazis, and members of the Greensboro police department jointly liable for the deaths of the activists.

The shooting and the trial outcomes left Greensboro divided and the Johnsons, particularly Nelson, ostracized. He and Joyce began attending church, and he became a pastor, embracing radical Christian love and liberation theology. With allies, the Johnsons founded the Beloved Community Center to advocate for economic, racial, and environmental justice, and Nelson started the Faith Community Church.

A citizen-based Truth and Reconciliation Commission investigated the 1979 shootings and concluded that "some [Greensboro police] officers had been deliberately absent," essentially allowing the murders to take place. After years of refusing to even read the commission's report, in 2020—due largely to the Johnsons' and others' tireless insistence—the Greensboro City Council apologized and launched annual social justice scholarships in the names of the five murdered activists: James Waller, Cesar Cauce, Sandra Smith, Michael Nathan, and William Sampson.

Nelson and Joyce Johnson have never stopped trying to solve the problems that brought them together in 1969.

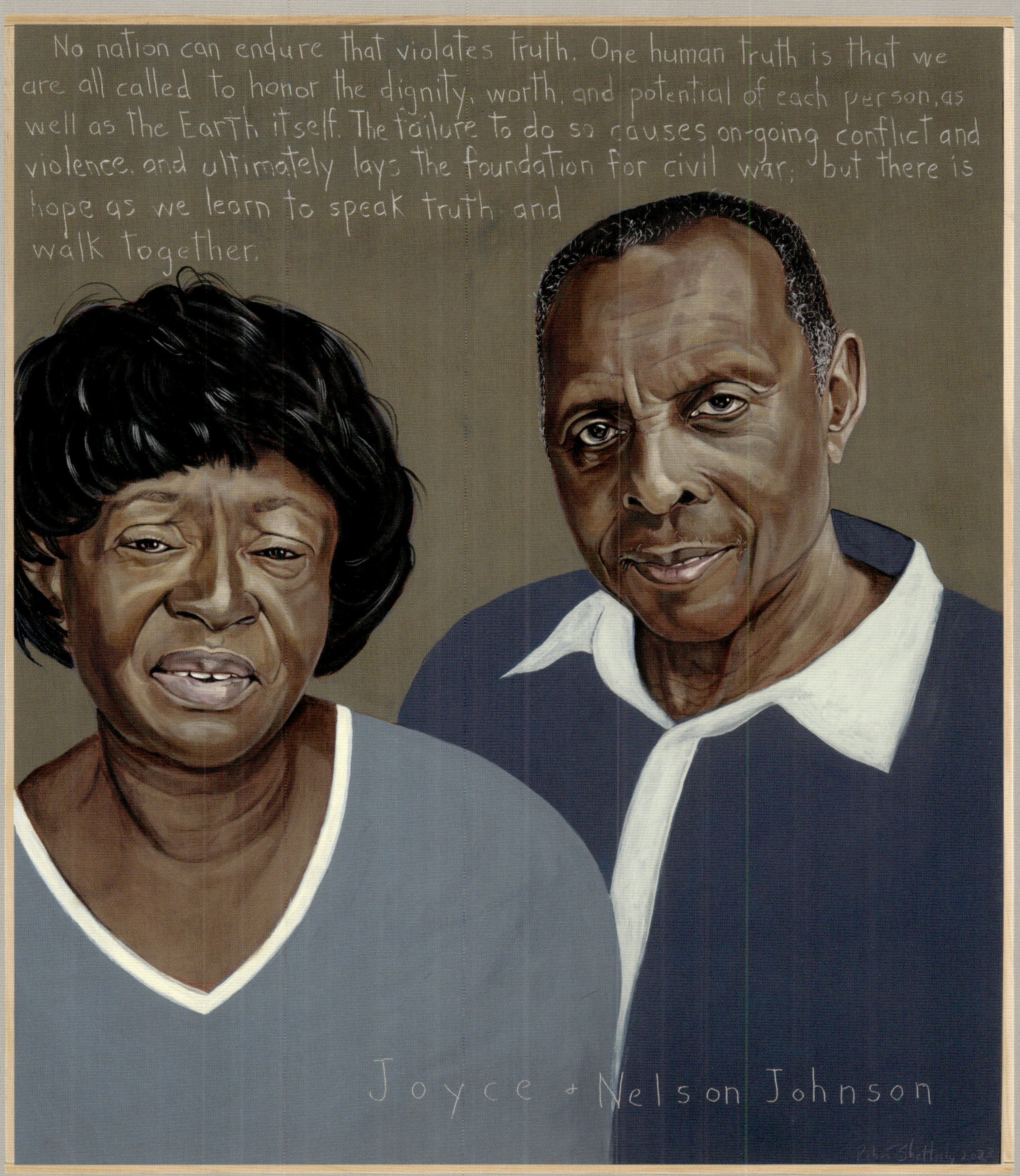

No nation can endure that violates truth. One human truth is that we are all called to honor the dignity, worth, and potential of each person, as well as the Earth itself. The failure to do so causes on-going conflict and violence, and ultimately lays the foundation for civil war; but there is hope as we learn to speak truth and walk together.
Joyce & Nelson Johnson

Maja Kazazic

War survivor, inspirational speaker, entrepreneur; b. 1977

*My life has helped me realize and understand the power of people. When we pull together
we can make anything happen—even world peace. We are all connected, our lives overlap,
our stories are intertwined, and our fates are shared.*

"Everyone gave me what they could, and together it formed a quilt of support that kept me going in those early difficult months." Maja Kazazic made this observation in 1993 after being hospitalized for a critical injury. Although suffering greatly at the time, she was able to create a metaphorical quilt from her personal story, transforming scraps and fragments of her trauma into a unified, beautiful whole.

The fashioning of Kazazic's life quilt began in Mostar, Bosnia-Herzegovina, in the late 1970s, where she enjoyed a halcyon childhood. She excelled in school and was passionate about becoming the best soccer player in Mostar and a professional athlete. Surrounded by a large and close-knit family of grandparents, aunts, uncles, and cousins, Maja was a typical teenager: "My friends wore T-shirts and jeans, watched *90210* and *Baywatch,* and listened to American music, like Billy Joel."

All that changed when the international armed conflict, the Bosnian War, came to Bosnia-Herzegovina in 1992. In mid-1993, Kazazic was critically injured by a mortar shell that killed six of her friends. Her lower legs and left hand were severely damaged, and a great deal of shrapnel entered her body, causing rapid blood loss. Over the next several months, Maja was treated at a makeshift facility near her home, where her left leg was amputated due to infection; at a hospital in Frankfurt, Germany; and then in Cumberland, Maryland. "[People] embraced me. Every group in town donated what I needed to live and what I needed to survive. The president of the hospital and my surgeons and nurses donated my medical care. Church groups provided housing, food, and clothing and gave me what they could."

Alone in a foreign land, not knowing English or American customs, sixteen-year-old Kazazic struggled with being away from her family and friends, but she learned to "take life on life's terms." She endured many more operations, learned English, and eventually began to walk with a prosthetic leg. She suffered from PTSD, then gained strength, confidence, and hope through her adoption of an amputee Great Dane named Rosie.

After graduating from St. Francis University in Loretto, Pennsylvania, with a degree in psychology, Kazazic became a website analyst and developer. Dozens of surgeries allowed her to play the occasional round of golf or set of tennis, but walking remained very difficult and painful. Her imperfect prosthesis prevented her from leading a more active and athletic life.

On one of her frequent visits to Clearwater Marine Aquarium, she observed a young dolphin, Winter, who had a prosthetic tail. The tail enabled Winter to swim like a normal dolphin. Kazazic contacted the company that made Winter's tail and within ten days had a new prosthetic, which enabled her to play golf and tennis, ride her bike, and walk long distances, pain-free.

A certified amputee peer counselor, Kazazic has helped recent amputees see that there is life after limb loss. She has volunteered at Camp No Limits for amputee children and Clearwater Marine Aquarium and has become a motivational speaker, inspiring others "to make sense of the chaos [and] live a purpose-driven life."

My life has helped me realize and understand the power of people. When we pull together, we can make anything happen — even world peace. We are all connected, our lives overlap, our stories are intertwined and our fates are shared.

Maja Kazazic

Robert Shetterly 2010

Kathy Kelly

Peace activist; b. 1952

At its core, war is impoverishment. War's genesis and ultimate end is in the poverty of our hearts.
If we can realize that the world's liberation begins within those troubled hearts,
then we may yet find peace. . . . What good has ever come from the slaughter of the innocent?

Kathy Kelly has been nominated for the Nobel Peace Prize three times. In 1996, she helped to found Voices in the Wilderness, a group that bore witness to the suffering the U.S./UN-imposed sanctions visited upon the people—especially the children—of Iraq. Then, from 2005 to 2020, she worked with Voices for Creative Nonviolence, an organization that continued and expanded the work, including opposition to U.S. economic and military warfare in the Middle East and challenges to drone warfare and the building of a U.S. military base in South Korea. Profiled by Katie Watson in *Hope* magazine (May/June 2003), Kelly traced her activism to her pious childhood on the South Side of Chicago. During high school she began to read about the Holocaust. "I remember thinking," she told Watson, "that I never ever-ever-ever want to be the person who is trying to be an innocent bystander while something that awful goes on."

After graduating from Loyola University and while still a graduate student at Chicago Theological Seminary, she volunteered at a soup kitchen run by a Catholic Worker house. This experience enabled her to convert the ideals derived from her studies into action. As a high school English teacher, as well as a committed antipoverty worker, she encouraged her students to make the same connections between theory and practice.

Kelly moved from addressing neighborhood poverty issues to advocating for nonviolence on a global scale. For her participation in planting corn in the soil above nuclear missile silos—a symbolic act intended to demonstrate the peaceful use of land—she was sentenced to nine months in federal prison. She said she found her jail term to be a "liberating" experience because it helped her to face the fear of coercion.

Kelly is no stranger to coercion. For refusing to pay federal income taxes, her teaching salary was garnished. For repeated visits to Iraq to distribute toys and medicine to children, she and her associates incurred thousands of dollars in fines, along with threats of imprisonment. When she trespassed at Fort Benning, Georgia, to protest the activities of the School of the Americas (now Western Hemisphere Institute for Security Cooperation) in 2003, she was arrested, physically and verbally abused, and sentenced to three months in federal prison. After such incarcerations, Kelly accepts the consequences of her actions, determined to stand against what Martin Luther King, Jr., called "the violence of desperate men."

In her later years, while still a very active advocate for nonviolence, Kelly has written numerous articles for both print and online magazines and coauthored two books. She tours the country speaking to schools, churches, and activist groups and has been awarded dozens of prizes, including the War Resisters League 2010 Peace Award, the U.S. Peace Memorial Foundation's 2015 Peace Prize, and the Veterans for Peace 2017 Gandhian Non-Violence Award.

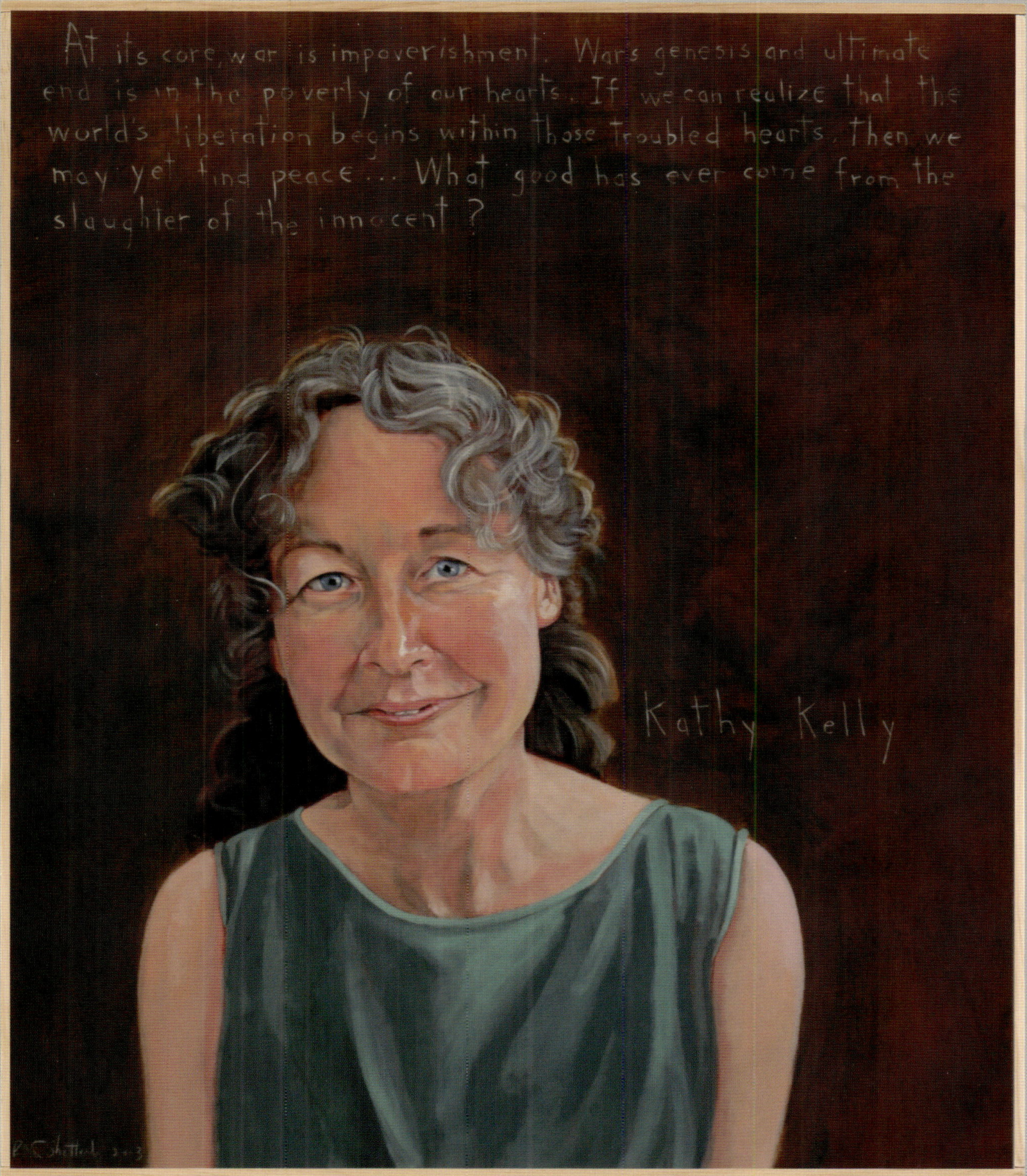

At its core, war is impoverishment. War's genesis and ultimate end is in the poverty of our hearts. If we can realize that the world's liberation begins within those troubled hearts, then we may yet find peace... What good has ever come from the slaughter of the innocent?

Kathy Kelly

Channapha Khamvongsa

Peace activist; b. 1973

The U.S. dropped 260 million cluster bombs on Laos during the Vietnam War. An estimated 80 million did not detonate, scattering throughout Lao villages, rice fields, school yards, pasture lands, and forests. The equivalent of a planeload of bombs was dropped every 8 minutes, 24 hours a day, for 9 years—more per capita than any other country in the world. This is called the Secret War. The mission of Legacies of War is to advocate for the clearance of unexploded bombs and provide space for healing the physical and emotional wounds of war.

Channapha Khamvongsa was born in Laos in 1973, when the country's civil war was ending. From June 1964 until June 1973, the United States had conducted what has become known as "the Secret War" in Laos, hidden from Americans and from Congress. Over the course of a decade, the U.S. military dropped more than two million tons of explosive devices on the country.

Many of these explosives failed to detonate and still litter the countryside of Lao People's Democratic Republic (Lao PDR). Even worse were the cluster bombs that open out at a predetermined height and spray a large quantity of cluster submunitions (or, in Laos, what are called "bombies") over the countryside. At a very minimum, 270,000,000 bombies were dropped on the country and about 30 percent, or 80,000,000, did not explode at that time. Most are still there today, awaiting a hapless farmer, traveler, jungle forager, or a curious child, to complete their murderous task. In the first twenty years of clearance, from 1994 to 2013, official efforts cleared half a million of these. At that rate, it would take 3,200 years to clear them all.

When Channapha was six years old, her family joined many others in crossing the Mekong River to the comparative safety of Thailand. Then they spent a year in a border refugee camp before being accepted for immigration to the United States and settling in Falls Creek, Virginia.

Growing up in the United States, Khamvongsa pursued her educational opportunities and in 2000 earned a bachelor's degree, followed by a master's in 2002. While working for the Ford Foundation in Washington, D.C., she met John Cavanagh, who had worked with the late Fred Branfman, editor of *Voices from the Plain of Jars*, a collection of stories written by Lao villagers who had suffered during the bombing. Khamvongsa's parents had not spoken to their children about their suffering in Laos. Now she discovered how the land of her ancestors was still covered in the unexploded detritus. These horrifying revelations led her to establish, in 2004, the nonprofit Legacies of War, dedicated to bringing relief to the people of Laos and pressuring the U.S. government to accept its responsibilities. Legacies of War gathered donations for unexploded ordnance clearance and victim assistance in Laos. Despite some lean years with sparse funding, Khamvongsa's extraordinary dedication, persistence, diplomacy, and networking skills kept Legacies alive

The pinnacle of her achievement came in September 2016, when President Obama visited Laos and announced that U.S. funding for the demining work would be doubled for each of the following three years. And, as he announced this, he acknowledged the pivotal work of Channapha Khamvongsa.

In 2019, Khamvongsa stepped away from the leadership role that she had played in Legacies and passed the mantle to others to carry on her remarkable work. Her legacy will be in the many lives she has saved from unexploded ordnance in the country of her birth.

The US dropped 260 million cluster bombs in Laos during the Vietnam War. An estimated 80 million did not detonate, scattering throughout Lao villages, rice fields, school yards, pasture lands, and forests. The equivalent of a planeload of bombs was dropped every 8 minutes, 24 hours a day, for 9 years — more per capita than any other country in the world. This is called the Secret War. The misson of Legacies of War is to advocate for the clearance of unexploded bombs and provide space for healing the physical and emotional wounds of war.

Channapha Khamvongsa

Ron Kovic

Antiwar and veterans rights activist; b. 1946

There is nothing in the lives of human beings more brutal and terrifying than war, and nothing more important than for those of us who have experienced it to share its awful truth.

Born on July 4, 1946, Ron Kovic grew up in Massapequa, New York, where he was raised to be a proud patriot in a family with a history of military service. Inspired by President John F. Kennedy's powerful words "Ask not what your country can do for you; ask what you can do for your country," Kovic signed up for the United States Marine Corps just a few months after his high school graduation.

He was deployed to Vietnam in December 1965. Many soldiers are frightened and confused when exposed to the speed and intensity of battle, and Kovic was no exception. On his second tour of duty, during a quick and confusing ambush by a North Vietnamese Army unit near a village along the Cua Viet River, he accidentally shot a young U.S. corporal. Then, during a night raid, Kovic and fellow soldiers were ordered to shoot into a small Vietnamese hut, where they believed enemy soldiers were hiding. But the hut had no enemies in it—only women and children left screaming, mangled, or dead. Kovic was horrified by these battlefield tragedies. On January 20, 1968, while leading his squad across an open area in the demilitarized zone north of the Cua Viet River, Kovic was shot, first in the right foot, then again through the right shoulder. He suffered a collapsed lung and a spinal cord injury that would leave him paralyzed from the chest down. Two marines who tried to save him died on the battlefield. The government awarded Kovic a Bronze Star with a *V* (denoting valor) and the Purple Heart for his service, courage, and injuries. But haunted by his experiences in war and adjusting to a life-changing injury, he took no solace in these accolades.

As Kovic looked back on his miserable time in the VA hospital, he was left "wondering how our government could spend so much money (billions of dollars) on the most lethal, technologically advanced weaponry to kill and maim human beings but not be able to take care of its own wounded when they came home." Paralyzed physically and tortured psychologically, Kovic had no answers to the questions he faced about war. However, he had a unique voice to share with audiences, and he began speaking out for peace at antiwar rallies and doing interviews on behalf of Vietnam Veterans of America.

Kovic attended the 1972 Republican National Convention. During President Nixon's acceptance speech, Kovic, from his wheelchair, famously told a reporter, "I'm a Vietnam veteran. I gave America my all, and the leaders of this government threw me and others away to rot in their VA hospitals. What's happening in Vietnam is a crime against humanity."

Four years later, Kovic again gained national attention at the Democratic National Convention, where he had been invited to speak, and he published his autobiography, *Born on the Fourth of July,* a searing account of his experiences in Vietnam and as a returning veteran. An award-winning film of the same name was released thirteen years later, with Tom Cruise starring as Kovic.

From his wheelchair, Ron Kovic has led many peaceful protest marches throughout the decades. In a world where films regularly glamorize war, Kovic symbolizes a different kind of war hero: a hero of truth, forgiveness, and peace.

There is nothing in the lives of human beings
more brutal and terrifying than war, and nothing more
important than for those of us who have experienced
it to share its awful truth.

Ron
Kovic

Dennis Kucinich

U.S. congressman, presidential candidate; b. 1946

Mr. Speaker, we make war with such certainty, yet are befuddled how to create peace. This paradox requires reflection if we are to survive. Making and endorsing war requires a secret love of death, a fearful desire to embrace annihilation. Creating peace requires compassion, putting ourselves in the other person's place, and all of their suffering and all of their hopes and to act from our heart's capacity to love, not fear.

Dennis Kucinich, former Democratic congressman from Ohio and two-time candidate for president, is an advocate for peace and a greener, healthier world. That he has carved out a successful political career holding true to these values is a remarkable achievement.

Kucinich's early life and career were lessons in persistence and hard work. He grew up in a large family that was constantly on the move, searching for affordable housing; occasionally they had to live out of the family car. Kucinich began his political career by running for Cleveland city council while he was still in college. In 1977, at the age of thirty-one, he became Cleveland's youngest mayor. His term was controversial. Kucinich refused to sell the city's publicly owned power company, Municipal Light, a decision so unpopular at the time that a contract was taken out on his life. It was years before the city recognized that Kucinich, in standing up to the banks and big businesses, had made the right decision.

Following the Municipal Light episode, Kucinich became a political pariah. But he restarted his political career, serving again as city councilman, then moving to the state senate, and finally to the U.S. House of Representatives in 1996. He remained in office until the end of 2012.

As a U.S. representative, Dennis Kucinich made a point of knowing and working for his constituency. He voted against the NAFTA agreement and the Patriot Act. He opposed the 2003 invasion of Iraq and received the U.S. Peace Memorial Foundation's 2010 Peace Prize "in recognition of his national leadership to prevent and end wars." He supported gay rights, including same-sex marriage, and a universal health care system. Kucinich also supported the Kyoto Protocol and domestic policies that address global warming and other conservation issues.

When he ran for president, Kucinich said that, if elected, he would create a Department of Peace, announcing that he was "going to let the rest of the world know that the days of America trying to be a nation above nations is over. We have to quit trying to dominate other countries, and we have to step out of our isolation and into the brotherhood and sisterhood of all people." As a candidate, Kucinich also said, "One of my proposals is to have millions of homes with wind and solar technologies. . . . In turn, you can create millions of jobs building alternative technologies."

Kucinich's ideas about how government can best serve the people do not always follow political party lines; often he stands alone. He keeps a small copy of the Constitution with him at all times to remind himself of Congress' commitment to upholding its principles. In 2008, Kucinich introduced an article to impeach President Bush for his deception in obtaining Congressional support for the invasion of Iraq.

Still interested in public service at age seventy-seven, Kucinich has announced his 2024 campaign for Ohio's 7th Congressional District as an independent. The heart of the matter, for Dennis Kucinich, is believing that "peace means being in harmony with nature." It shapes his life and his work for a greener and more socially just America.

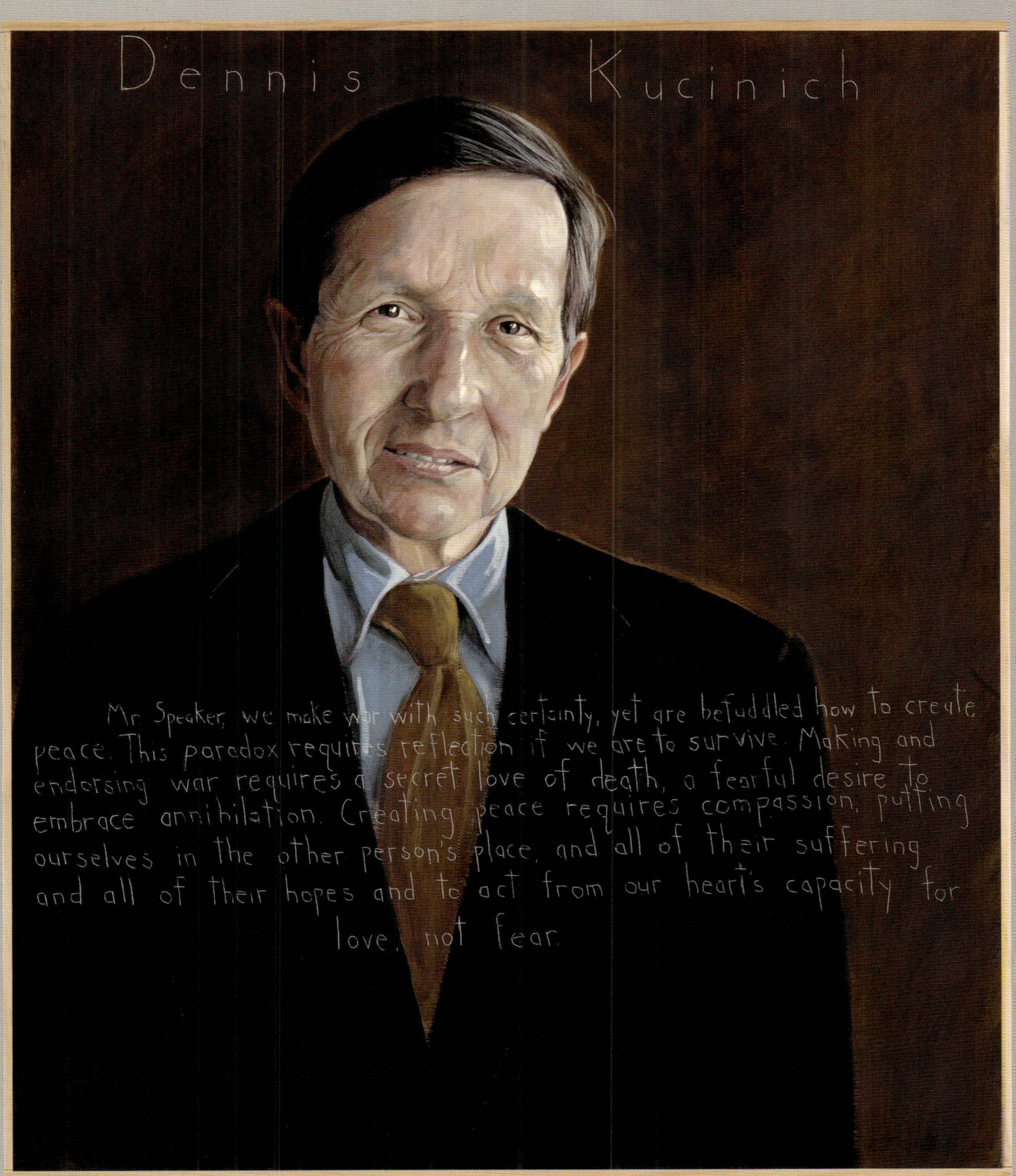

Dennis   Kucinich

Mr. Speaker, we make war with such certainty, yet are befuddled how to create
peace. This paradox requires reflection if we are to survive. Making and
endorsing war requires a secret love of death, a fearful desire to
embrace annihilation. Creating peace requires compassion, putting
ourselves in the other person's place, and all of their suffering
and all of their hopes and to act from our heart's capacity for
love, not fear.

Dr. Bernard Lown

Medical pioneer, peace activist, humanitarian; b.1921, d. 2021

Securing a future free of genocidal weapons requires above all eliminating the political and economic inequities that sunder rich and poor countries. As the Berlin Wall divided East and West, so inequality now creates a fracturing divide that augurs global chaos, terrorism, and war.

From pioneering advancements in the treatment of cardiovascular disease to becoming one of the world's most influential nuclear disarmament activists, Dr. Bernard Lown was committed to "behaving as though the destiny of our world depends on each of our actions. This is the moral imperative of our age."

In 1935, at the age of fourteen, Lown emigrated with his parents from Lithuania to the United States to avoid Nazi persecution. They settled in Lewiston, Maine, where his father found work with relatives who owned a shoe factory. In 1937, Lown witnessed a policeman arresting an unconscious, bleeding shoe factory striker who had been severely beaten, while allowing his strike-breaking assailant to walk free. Jeopardizing his relationship with his family, Lown joined the striking workers. "I have retained a permanent sense of outrage against such unfairness and injustice ever since. . . ."

During high school, yet to master English, he was mocked by fellow students and derided by his English teacher as "a bumbling idiot." He gained admittance to the University of Maine on a trial basis. The dean commented that if he worked hard, he might prove to be a C student. Lown graduated summa cum laude, with a B.S in zoology.

After completing his training at Johns Hopkins University School of Medicine, Lown quickly ascended the ranks of medicine and academia to become a professor of cardiology at the Harvard School of Public Health and a senior physician at Brigham and Women's Hospital. Throughout his career, Lown pioneered major medical breakthroughs, while challenging unfair aspects of the system and urging more humane and equitable treatment of patients.

In 1961, inspired by Philip Noel-Baker, a nuclear disarmament advocate, Lown formed Physicians for Social Responsibility (PSR), a group of Boston-area colleagues, to study the consequences of a nuclear attack. Lown firmly believed that the Cold War was perpetuated by fear. "In an unstable climate of terror, feeling besieged by a foe without scruple leads to a state of jumbled intellectual incoherence, blocking the only exit: meaningful dialogue between adversaries." Essential to the creation of such dialogue was the friendship between two of the world's most esteemed cardiologists: Yevgeni Chazov of the Soviet Union and Bernard Lown. Their working relationship and friendship laid the groundwork for cooperation and enabled the formation of the International Physicians for the Prevention of Nuclear War (IPPNW). In December of 1985, Lown and Chazov accepted the Nobel Peace Prize on behalf of IPPNW.

In October 1988, the bridge that connects the towns of Lewiston and Auburn, Maine, was dedicated as the Bernard Lown Peace Bridge—the very same bridge where violent confrontation of the Lewiston-Auburn shoe strike took place. Lown said, ". . . the naming of a bridge is emblematic of my life. My aim was always to connect. To connect the doctor with the patient, . . . a Soviet with an American, the rich world with the poor world. . . . We must be able to bequeath to our children the most fundamental of all rights . . . the right to survival."

Securing a future free of genocidal weapons requires
above all eliminating the political and economic inequities
that sunder rich and poor countries. As the Berlin wall divided
East and West, so inequality now creates a fracturing divide
that augurs global chaos, terrorism, and war.

Dr. Bernard Lown

Robert Shetterly 2024

Colman McCarthy

Journalist, developer of peace studies curriculum; b. 1938

Give peace a chance, yes, but why not get serious and give it a place in the curriculum: peace courses in every school, every grade, every nation. Unless we teach our children peace, someone else will teach them violence.

When Colman McCarthy left *The Washington Post* in 1998, after nearly thirty years as a columnist, he had another full-time job lined up—teaching peace in America's classrooms and lecture halls. He'd started teaching peace part-time in 1982 and by 2011 had instructed more than ten thousand students in what he calls "the other side" of the story. "I've been accused of teaching a one-sided course," he wrote in *The Nation.* "*Perhaps,* except that my course *is* the other side, the one that students aren't getting in conventional history or political science courses, which present violent militaristic solutions as rational and necessary."

Despite many schools' resistance to the idea, peace education is growing. Back in 1970, there was a single college program in peace studies in the United States; by 2011, there were more than five hundred.

When McCarthy addresses a new audience, he likes to ask how many present have taken a peace course. Few, if any, hands go up. "If this were a peace-loving, peace-seeking and peace-building society, every hand would have gone up. We all graduate as peace illiterates," he says.

Born in Glen Head, New York, in 1938, McCarthy graduated from the Jesuit-affiliated Spring Hill College in Mobile, Alabama, and then spent five years in a Trappist monastery. When he began his career in journalism, he decided to be a peace correspondent instead of a war correspondent. He began by covering Martin Luther King, Jr., in the summer of 1966 and went on to interview many prominent peace activists, including Nobel Peace Prize winners Archbishop Desmond Tutu, Mother Teresa, Ireland's Mairead

Corrigan and Seán MacBride, Argentina's Pérez Esquivel, and Muhammad Yunus of Bangladesh.

His first foray into the classroom was at School Without Walls, a public high school in Washington, D.C. He established a motto for the class: "Instead of asking questions, be bolder and question the answers." The most heavily promoted answer to the question is that violence leads to peace. "If violence were truly effective," says McCarthy, "we would have had peace eons ago."

Instead of the "necessity" of war, McCarthy talks about the victories of peace: the successful non-violent movements against Marcos in the Philippines, Pinochet in Chile, Milosevic in Yugoslavia, and Shevardnadze in Georgia; Lech Walesa's efforts in Poland; Nelson Mandela in South Africa; Vaclav Havel becoming president in Czechoslovakia. "And so there's proof that, as Martin Luther King said, if non-violent resistance is well organized, it can be far more effective than violence."

McCarthy married Mavourneen Deegan, a nurse, in 1967. Together they founded the Center for Teaching Peace in 1985. He lectures widely and has taught peace in many schools and universities over the past twenty-five years. McCarthy's books include *All of One Peace* (1994) and *I'd Rather Teach Peace* (2002). He was awarded an Alicia Patterson Journalism Fellowship in 1998 and is a recipient of the Peace Abbey Courage of Conscience Award and the El-Hibri Peace Education Prize, among others.

McCarthy, a vegan, is also an animal rights advocate. His primary mode of transportation is a bicycle, on which he has passed the 100,000-mile mark.

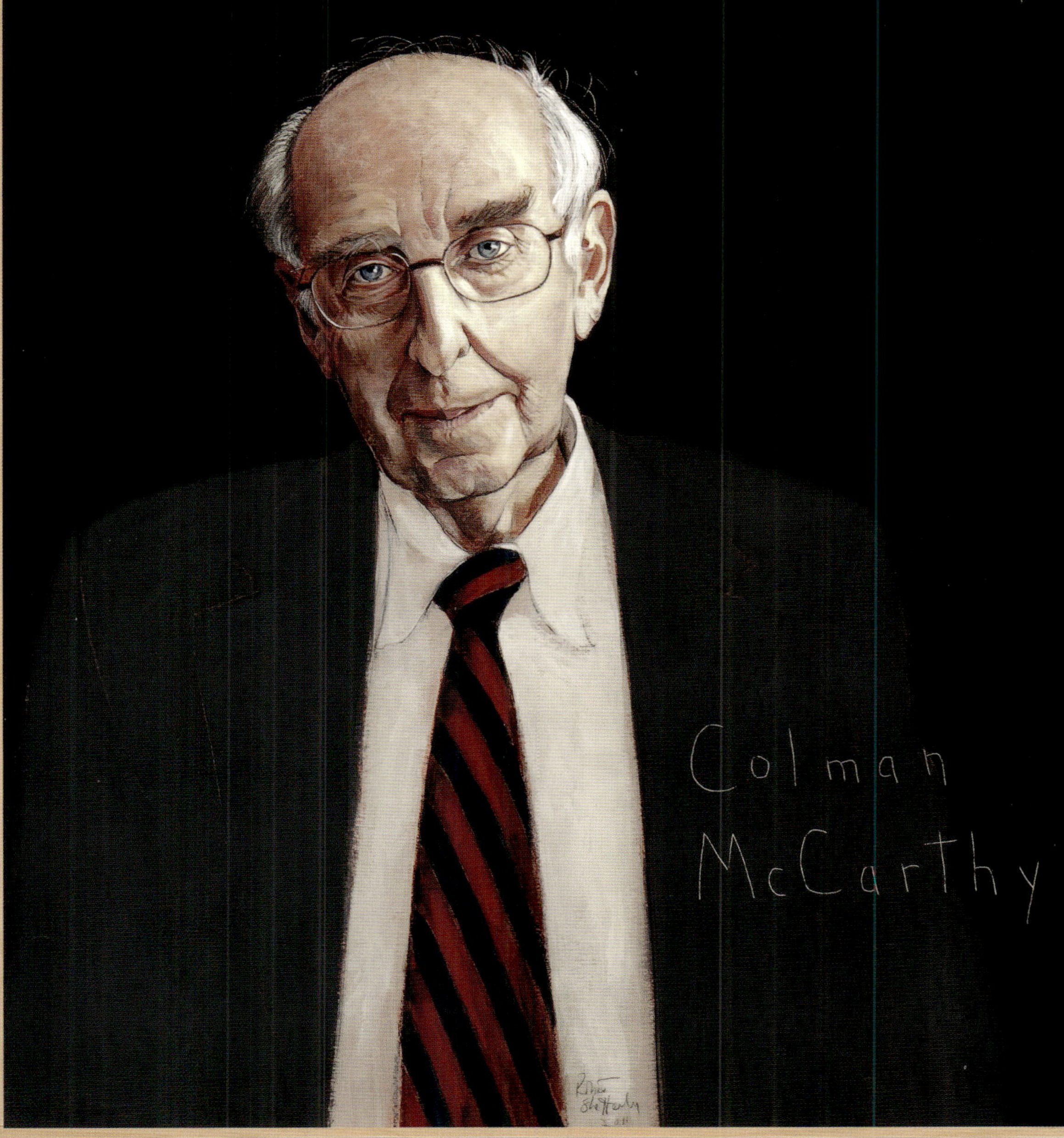
Give peace a chance, yes, but why not get serious and give it
a place in the curriculum: peace courses in every school, every
grade, every nation. Unless we teach our children peace, someone
else will teach them violence.

Colman
McCarthy

Ray McGovern

Retired CIA officer; b. 1939

Allegations keep cropping up in the press that CIA alumni are undermining the Bush/Cheney administration. In at least one sense, I suppose, this is true. For when an administration embarks on a war justified by little or no intelligence, speaking the truth can be regarded as treachery. The country could use more of that kind of "treachery."

Ray McGovern is an activist who writes and lectures about, among other issues, war and the role of the CIA. He holds a master's degree in Russian Studies from Fordham University, a certificate in theological studies from Georgetown University, and is a graduate of Harvard Business School's Advanced Management Program.

In 1996, McGovern caught the attention of the media when he criticized the Pope's position on women priests. Later, his analysis of the war in Iraq, and of the CIA's role in instigating that war, made McGovern one of the country's most powerful anti-war voices.

"And ye shall know the truth and the truth shall make you free." Those words are carved into the marble facade of the entrance to the CIA. McGovern worked to adhere to this credo during his twenty-seven-year career as a CIA analyst, understanding the inscription to mean that "the primary function of the Central Intelligence Agency is to seek the truth . . . and to be able to report that truth without fear or favor."

McGovern's intelligence work, beginning in the U.S. Army and continuing at the CIA, spanned seven presidents, from President Kennedy to President George H. W. Bush. As an analyst on foreign policy, McGovern synthesized daily intelligence and then briefed senior White House advisers with his conclusions. Now retired, McGovern is proud of the fact that he reported his findings "without fear or favor" to the politicians and was supported in his work by his superiors.

As a cofounder of Veteran Intelligence Professionals for Sanity (VIPS), McGovern speaks out against what he sees as corruption in the CIA, which allowed the agency's integrity to bend to the will of President George W. Bush and his White House officials. He asserts that the war in Iraq was manufactured and sold to the United States under false pretenses—the real reason being oil. In a 2007 letter to former CIA Director George Tenet, McGovern and other former intelligence officers called Tenet on the carpet for signing documents he knew to be fraudulent—one, for example, that stated that Iraq was buying uranium from Africa. They also called him out for testifying that Iraq had links to Al-Qaeda, when actual intelligence reports found no link between Iraq and Osama bin Laden. In short, they accused Tenet of "dovetailing" intelligence to fit with what politicians wanted to hear in the push for an unnecessary war with Iraq.

During both the Bush and Obama years, the White House considered an attack on Iran to stop its apparent development of nuclear capabilities. McGovern raised concerns over why an attack would be necessary, writing, "The very same men who . . . brought us the war in Iraq are now focusing on Iran, which they view as the only remaining obstacle to American domination of the entire oil-rich Middle East."

He also called for the impeachment of President George W. Bush and Vice President Dick Cheney for electronic eavesdropping on Americans without a judicial warrant.

When McGovern retired in 1990, he received the CIA's Intelligence Commendation Medal. He returned the medal in 2006, in protest of the CIA's secret use of torture. He continues to live by the adage "And ye shall know the truth, and the truth shall make you free."

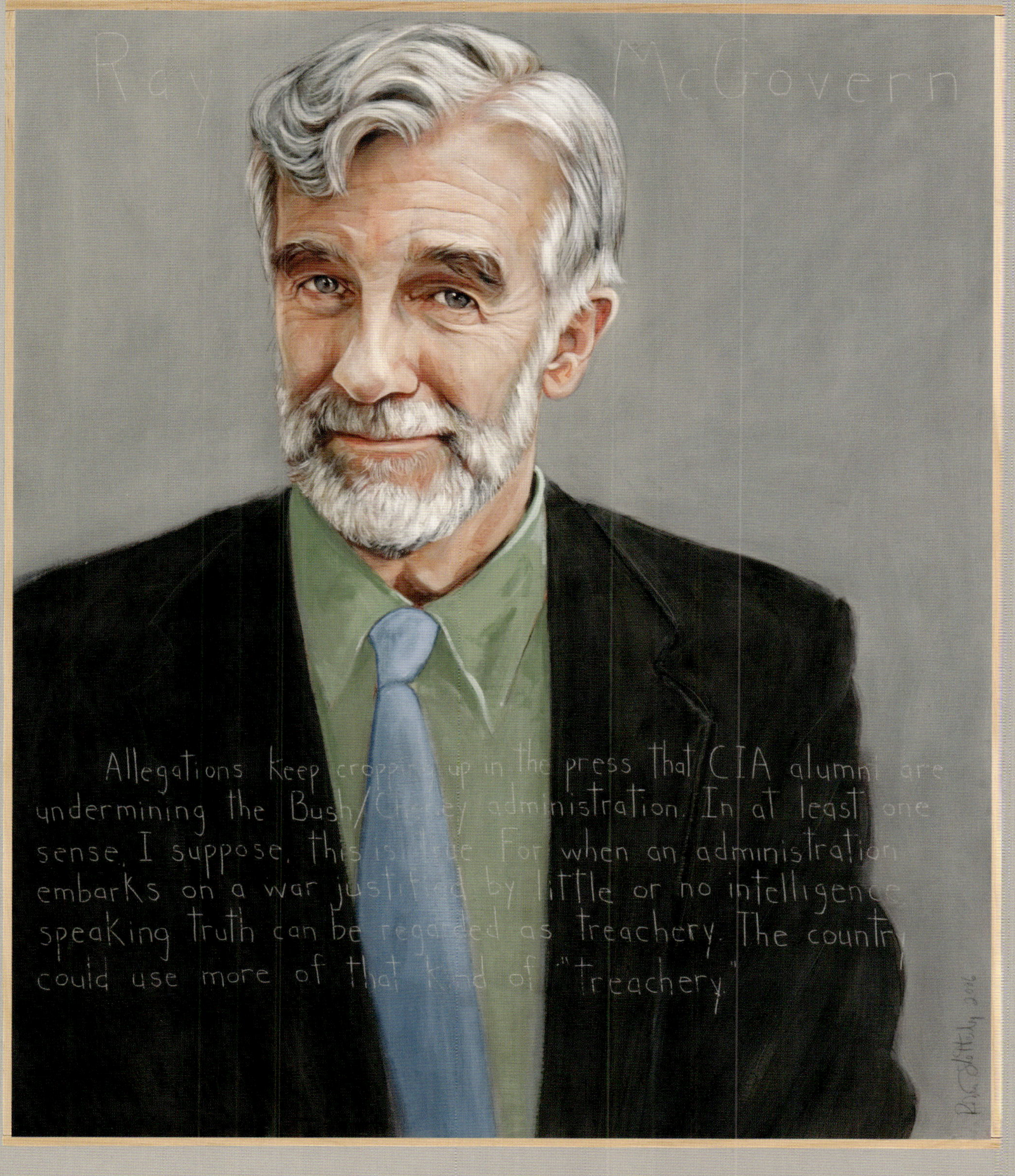
Ray McGovern
Allegations keep cropping up in the press that CIA alumni are undermining the Bush/Cheney administration. In at least one sense, I suppose, this is true. For when an administration embarks on a war justified by little or no intelligence, speaking truth can be regarded as treachery. The country could use more of that kind of "treachery."

Camilo Mejía

Soldier, war resister, peace activist; b. 1975

I was a coward not for leaving the war, but for having been a part of it in the first place. . . . I failed to fulfill my moral duty as a human being, and instead I chose to fulfill my duty as a soldier. . . . What good is freedom if we are not able to live with our own actions? I am confined to a prison, but I feel, today more than ever, connected to all humanity. Behind these bars I sit a free man because I listened to a higher power, the voice of my conscience.

Camilo Mejía was born in Managua, Nicaragua, in 1975. His family moved to Costa Rica and then to the United States. He finished high school in New York City. Mejía never applied for nor received U.S. citizenship. Nevertheless, he went to college at the University of Miami on a military-funded scholarship, intending to major in psychology and Spanish. But, in the spring of 2003, before he had finished college, the military sent Mejía to Iraq, where he spent five months in active combat, and then to Jordan, where he spent two more months.

In late 2003, he came home on furlough and realized he could not go back: "Going home gave me the opportunity to put my thoughts in order and to listen to what my conscience had to say. . . . I thought of the suffering of a people whose country was in ruins and who were further humiliated by the raids, patrols and curfews of an occupying army. And I realized that none of the reasons we were told about why we were in Iraq turned out to be true. . . . I realized that I was part of a war that I believed was immoral and criminal, a war of aggression, a war of imperial domination. I realized that acting upon my principles became incompatible with my role in the military, and I decided that I could not return to Iraq." He filed for conscientious objector status and told the military he refused to return to the battlefield.

In May 2004, Mejía was convicted of desertion by the U.S. military—a charge that can be punishable by death—and he was sentenced to a year in jail. He served his time at Fort Sill military prison in Oklahoma. During his incarceration, Amnesty International recognized him as a prisoner of conscience and the activist organization Refuse and Resist gave him its Courageous Resister Award.

After his release in February 2005, Mejía devoted his time to speaking out against the war in Iraq and encouraging others to understand that being a part of an immoral war was more cowardly than breaking the law. His book, *The Road from Ar Ramadi: The Private Rebellion of Staff Sergeant Camilo Mejía* (2007), details his personal journey. He served on the board of the nonprofit organization Iraq Veterans Against the War (now About Face: Veterans Against the War). For his work, he received Global Exhange's Young Leader Award and the Peace Abbey Courage of Conscience Award.

Mejía says that becoming a war resister does not take anything special, just the belief that one person can make a difference: "Many have called me a coward, others have called me a hero. I believe I can be found somewhere in the middle. To those who have called me a hero, I say that I don't believe in heroes, but I believe that ordinary people can do extraordinary things."

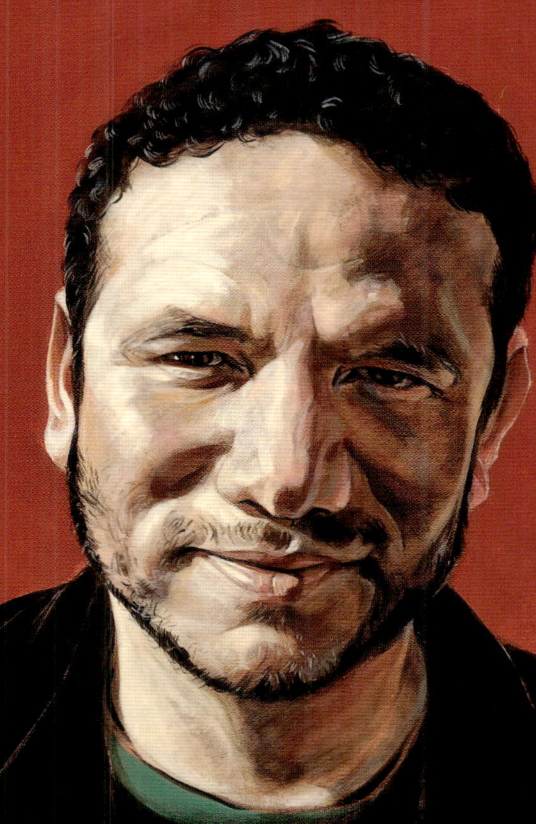

I was a coward, not for leaving the war, but for having been a part of it in the first place... I failed to fulfill my moral duty as a human being, and instead I chose to fulfill my duty as a soldier... What good is freedom if we are not able to live with our own actions? I am confined to a prison, but I feel, today more than ever, connected to all humanity.

Camilo Mejía

Behind these bars I sit a free man because I listened to a higher power: the voice of my conscience.

Jeannette Rankin

Suffragist, congresswoman, pacifist; b. 1880, d. 1973

Women remind me of the cows on our ranch in Montana. A cow has a calf and after a while some man comes along and takes the calf away. She bawls for a while, then goes on and has another calf. . . . If we had 10,000 women willing to go to prison that would end the war. We've had 10,000 women sit back and let their sons be killed.

The eldest child of a Montana rancher and a schoolteacher, Jeannette Rankin would cast a vote in Congress for peace before most American women were allowed to vote. After graduating from Montana State University, Rankin taught school, designed furniture, and dabbled in social work. Then the women's suffrage movement ignited her passion, and she became legislative secretary of the National American Woman Suffrage Association. Her efforts led to women in Montana winning the right to vote in 1914, five years before the Nineteenth Amendment guaranteed that right nationally.

In 1916, Rankin was elected to the U.S. Congress as a Republican. Just four days into her term, she drew national attention by voting—together with forty-nine men—against the U.S. entry into World War I. "I want to stand with my country, but I cannot vote for war," she said. She later voted for suffrage, civil liberties, equal pay, and child welfare, but her antiwar vote kept her from being reelected in 1920.

Working for peace became Rankin's life work. "There can be no compromise with war," she wrote. "[I]t cannot be reformed or controlled; cannot be disciplined into decency or codified into common sense, for war is the slaughter of human beings, temporarily regarded as enemies, on as large a scale as possible." She held leadership roles in the Women's International League for Peace and Freedom and other advocacy groups, and she later traveled to India to learn about nonviolence from Gandhi.

In 1940, Rankin ran for Congress on an isolationist platform, and Montana again sent her to Washington. After the attack on Pearl Harbor, she was the only member of Congress to vote against declaring war on Japan. Although editor William Allen White disagreed with her position, he wrote, "Probably a hundred men in Congress would have liked to do what she did. Not one of them had the courage to do it."

In 1968 and again in 1970, just days before her ninetieth birthday, Rankin went to Washington, D.C., to lead marches against the Vietnam War.

Jeannette Rankin

Women remind me of the cows on our ranch in Montana. A cow has a calf and after a while some man comes along and takes the calf away. She bawls for awhile, then goes on and has another calf. If we had 10,000 women willing to go to prison that would end the war. We've had 10,000 women sit back and let their sons be killed.

Robert Shetterly 2005

Alice Rothchild

Physician, author, Israel-Palestine peace activist, filmmaker; b. 1948

Where are the protests from political organizations, the cries of horror from U.S. ministers as well as rabbis and mainstream Jewish community groups who cry "Never again!" Surely history will teach us that Israel cannot claim a special moral dispensation because of past suffering, and then behave immorally. Misusing the term anti-Semitism to characterize criticism of Israeli behavior ultimately renders the term meaningless.

Alice Rothchild was born in Boston, Massachusetts, in 1948, the same year that the First Arab-Israeli War erupted and the State of Israel was established. Her parents were first-generation American Jews who created a "Jewish family with a deep love of Israel and a profound understanding of the horrors of the Holocaust." Seymour Rothchild, her father, was a self-made man, a chemist. Her mother, Sylvia Rothchild, wrote *Voices from the Holocaust,* chronicling the oral histories of Nazi Holocaust survivors.

Sylvia's interest in history and individual narratives would have a profound impact on her daughter's exploration of divisions between Israel and Palestine. "Immersed in these stories, I began to understand that buried in the wounds of my own people's near annihilation, another people's story was lost," says Dr. Rothchild. ". . . I feel it is my personal responsibility as my mother's daughter and as a Jewish American who has grappled with the multiple narratives in this region to listen and document the tragedy that was created by my own people's tragedy."

During Alice's childhood, the family visited her Orthodox grandparents in Brooklyn, New York, to share Jewish holidays. Alice attended Hebrew School and participated in an early version of a Bat Mitzvah at a local conservative synagogue. She graduated from Bryn Mawr College in 1970 with a bachelor's degree in psychology and subsequently attended Boston University School of Medicine. Her interest in progressive politics began in the 1960s and 1970s, when she participated in campus opposition to the Vietnam War; later, she committed herself to the feminist and health-reform movements.

It wasn't until 1997, through her involvement with the Boston Workmen's Circle, that Alice turned much of her nonmedical focus to learning and writing about the Israeli-Palestinian conflict and its relationship to U.S. foreign policy. She learned that each year millions of dollars are spent on media to promote aggressively an Israel-right-or-wrong political stand, while the Palestinian side of the story is being discredited by this activist media.

Rothchild cofounded American Jews for a Just Peace–Boston. Since then, she has worked with a number of local and national groups and is now active with Jewish Voice for Peace, the Gaza Mental Health Foundation, Just World Educational, and We Are Not Numbers.

Rothchild's first book *Broken Promises, Broken Dreams: Stories of Jewish and Palestinian Trauma and Resilience* (2007) has been followed by several written works, including a young adult novel *Finding Melody Sullivan* (2023) and a documentary film *Voices Across the Divide* (2013). Her memoir *Inspired and Outraged: The Making of a Feminist Physician* is due to be published in 2024.

Apart from her activism, Alice is a board-certified obstetrician-gynecologist. Among a long list of professional positions, she has served on the staff of Beth Israel Hospital (now Beth Israel Deaconess Medical Center) and as an assistant professor of obstetrics, gynecology, and reproductive biology at Harvard Medical School. Now retired from clinical practice, Rothchild writes, lectures, and maintains a regular blog..

Dr. Alice Rothchild

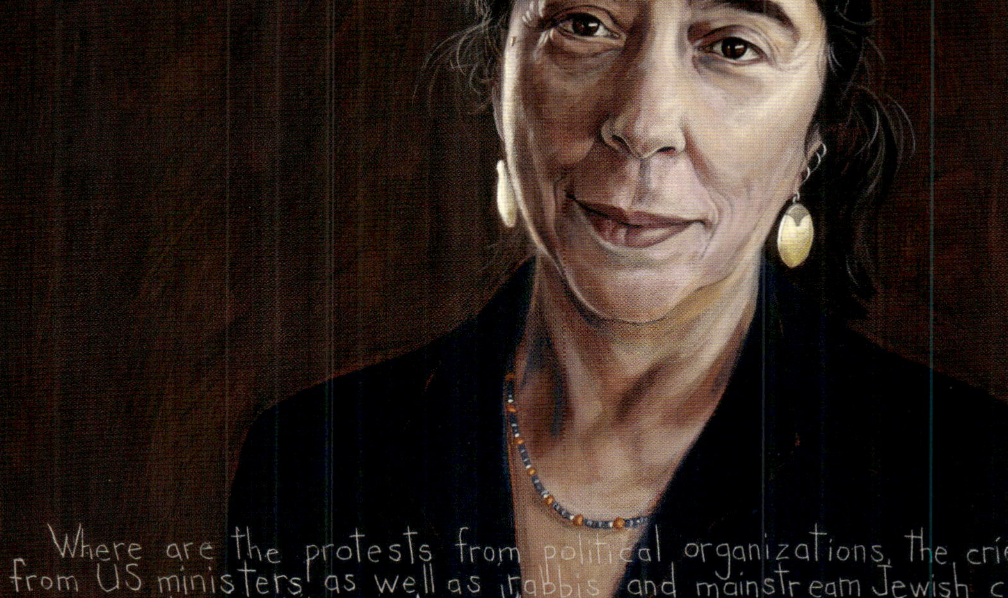

Where are the protests from political organizations, the cries of horror
from US ministers as well as rabbis, and mainstream Jewish community
groups who cry "Never Again!"

Surely history will teach us that Israel cannot claim a special moral
dispensation because of past suffering, and then behave immorally.

Misusing the term anti-Semitism to characterize criticism of Israeli
behavior ultimately renders the term meaningless.

Kali Rubaii

Cultural anthropologist, anti-imperialist; b. 1987

Liberal democratic empires frame imperial terror as "defense" and the self-defense of targeted people as "terrorism." While the US empire may speak of the sanctity of life, its implementation centers on the sanctity of lethal force, not only by bombs and bullets, but also by triggering a cascade of public health crises and ecological collapse.

In 2003, the United States invaded Iraq for the second time since 1991, after a decade of imposing deadly sanctions. This Second Gulf War, launched as part of the Global War on Terrorism, killed over 300,000 Iraqi people. According to the watchdog organization Costs of War, the 2003 U.S. invasion left 9.2 million Iraqis internally displaced or as refugees.

The survivors suffer ongoing destruction: Air, water, soil, and bodies are saturated with toxins, not only from bombings but also from deregulated postwar industry. Basic health-sustaining infrastructure, including the country's relatively robust medical system, was leveled and remains at minimal capacity. Perhaps most destructive of all were the 100 Orders, policies drafted by the United States to restructure and privatize every sector of Iraq's economy, thereby gutting the country of its own resources.

These by-products of war are what Dr. Kali Rubaii, a cultural anthropologist, sees during her visits to Fallujah, Ramadi, and the rural communities of Anbar Province. Through forensic ethnography, Dr. Rubaii's work bears witness to the environmental and health impacts of U.S. wars in Iraq and the extractive industries that fuel them.

Coordinating with farmers, researchers, doctors, and environmental activists, Rubaii documents the links between the epidemic of birth defects in Fallujah and military environmental damage, including collapsed infrastructure, exposure to metals like depleted uranium and lead, and chronic displacement. She also investigates the concrete industry's complicity in militarizing Iraq's landscape and poisoning the air and waterways of the Bazian Valley. She has followed transnational mineral mining in Africa to weapons manufacturing in North America to munitions recycling in the Middle East—a supply cycle that exposes many communities to metals and by-products, increasing risks of cancer and reproductive harm.

Rubaii has also called attention to Iraqi civilians' exposure to U.S. military burn pits—open-air combustion of trash, including industrial chemicals, medical and human waste, munitions, tanks, uniforms, and e-waste. She notes, "While toxic, burn pits are the least of people's problems; they symbolize the toxic relationship the US has had with Iraq for decades. In Fallujah, it is not uncommon to hear from people who remember being tortured or maliciously treated by American soldiers, who had their homes destroyed more than once, who experience a very high number of miscarriages or stillbirths, who lived in a tent while displaced, who breathed in smoke from missile strikes, and who saw dead bodies floating down the Euphrates. The levels of violence—from the substances in the earth to the unnamed dead in the water—are not going away. This soil will not forget: with every sandstorm, people inhale the past of war."

Rubaii is also cofounder, with Debra Ellis and Ross Caputi, of the Islah Reparations Project. For over a decade, the organization has channeled grassroots reparations from individual Americans to victims, primarily in Iraq. Islah has worked to accelerate resettlement for the displaced, facilitated medical treatment for those who face barriers to treatment, and supported grassroots community efforts to restore public spaces like skate parks and youth programs.

Liberal democratic empires frame imperial terror as "defense" and the self-defense of targeted people as "terrorism." While the US empire may speak of the sanctity of life, its implementation centers on the sanctity of lethal force, not only by bombs and bullets, but also by triggering a cascade of public health crises and ecological collapse.

Kali
Rubaii

Ben Salmon

Conscientious objector; b. 1888, d. 1932

There is no such animal as a just war.

As a young boy, Ben Salmon loved to hike the hills with his family west of Denver. He learned respect for all of nature from his father, a vegetarian, who taught Ben that no living creature should be killed.

Many years later, imprisoned for his anti-militarism, he wrote, "As a young boy, I was quite a patriot. . . . One time, I was in a play, and much to my delight, I was chosen as a soldier. I was about ten years old. I prized my uniform more than I did my life. I learned to sing patriotic songs, I read war books, and when the soldiers marched off for Spain [1898] I was brokenhearted to think that I could not go with them." Ben also noted how conflicted he was as he learned that the Old Testament commandment "Thou shalt not kill" was reinforced by the New Testament teaching "Love your enemies."

Ben left school at age fourteen to work in a print shop. Learning to type, he soon had good-paying jobs as a clerk who recognized workplace and economic injustices. He had become a socialist and was fired by a railroad company for union organizing. He created a newsletter that he gave away in the streets, espousing socialism to address capitalism's economic injustices. He ran for a state office as a Democrat and "single tax" candidate and lost.

In April 1914, after a miners' union strike, the Colorado National Guard and private guards from the Colorado Fuel and Iron Company massacred children, women, and men southwest of Denver. The Ludlow Massacre had a profound effect on Salmon. For his newsletter, he wrote an article entitled "THOU SHALL NOT KILL" and quoted Jack London, who wrote, "Young man, the lowest aim in your life is to become a soldier."

When the United States declared war on Germany, Salmon wrote a letter to President Wilson, saying, "[A]ll men are my brothers. The commandment 'Thou shall not kill' is unconditional and inexorable." Although Salmon was exempt from military service as a married man with a pregnant wife and a widowed mother, he refused to sign a government conscription questionnaire. He was found guilty of desertion (even though he was not in the military) and guilty of propagandizing for publicly sharing his letter to the president. The military judge sentenced him to twenty-five years hard labor.

Salmon was shuffled in chains to seven different federal prisons, often placed in solitary confinement in small, damp, rat-infested basement cells. He went on a 133-day hunger strike. The military feared he would die and generate public criticism, so they strapped him to a gurney several times a day, shoved a ceramic funnel down his throat, and fed him milk to keep him alive.

Almost two years after the war had ended, Salmon, emaciated from months on the hunger strike, his throat raw from forced feeding, was sent by train from Utah to a federal insane asylum, St. Elizabeth's, in Washington, D.C. Released on Thanksgiving in 1920, Salmon could not return safely to his Denver home. *The Denver Post* had labeled him a "coward with a yellow strip down his back," and he received death threats.

Salmon settled in Chicago, where his wife and young son joined him in 1921. Struggling from the trauma of his prison treatment, Salmon died in 1932; he was only forty-three years old. When his unmarked grave was discovered in 2016. friends of Salmon laid a simple grave marker inscribed "THERE IS NO SUCH THING AS A JUST WAR." BEN J. SALMON.

Ben Salmon
There is no such animal as a   just war.

Cindy Sheehan

Mother, antiwar activist; b. 1957

George . . . your reckless and wanton foreign policies killed my son, Spc. Casey Austin Sheehan, in the illegal and unjust war on Iraq. . . . Helping to bring about your political downfall will be the most noble accomplishment of my life, and it will bring justice for my son and the hundreds of other brave Americans and tens of thousands of innocent Iraqis your lies have killed.

Cindy Lee Miller was born on July 10, 1957. She married Patrick Sheehan and the couple had four children—Casey, Carly, Andy, and Jane. The whole family was active in their church; Sheehan was once a youth minister. They were a tight-knit family that, in Sheehan's words, "did everything together."

Sheehan's world changed forever when, on an April 4, 2004, mission in Sadr City, Iraq, Army Specialist Casey Sheehan, her oldest child, was killed. Sheehan and other military families met with President George W. Bush in June 2004. By October, Sheehan's grief had led her to action. She wrote, "I was ashamed that I hadn't tried to stop the war before Casey died. . . . Well, I now felt that if I couldn't make a difference, I would at least try."

Sheehan became one of the strongest, most personal and persistent voices in the movement against the war in Iraq. Her quest to end the war, bring soldiers home, and hold politicians accountable for the decisions that sent the troops to Iraq in the first place was indefatigable.

The American Friends Service Committee created a traveling exhibition of combat boots, each pair representing a U.S. military casualty. They invited Sheehan to speak at the opening of the exhibit, titled "Eyes Wide Open: The Human Cost of War," which coincided with President George W. Bush's second inauguration, in January 2005. At that event, Sheehan got the idea to start an organization called Gold Star Families for Peace.

In early August 2005, Sheehan—or "Peace Mom," as she came to be called—camped in a ditch near President Bush's ranch in Crawford, Texas. She requested a second personal meeting with the president, who had declared that the fallen soldiers had died for a "noble cause." Sheehan wanted to know exactly what that cause was and demanded an immediate end to what she viewed as an unjust and immoral war.

So many people stopped by to show their support or join her camp that her demonstration became known as "Camp Casey." A few days later, one of Bush's neighbors offered the Camp Casey participants some land to use as their base. Camp Casey became a regular protest event, popping up when President Bush was in Crawford for holidays and vacations.

Between Camp Casey operations, Sheehan traveled extensively to join antiwar rallies and to meet with activists and leaders from around the world. She is credited with having revived the antiwar protest and being the face for the peace and justice movement. Her published works include an account of her first year of activism, entitled *Not One More Mother's Child* (2005); a collection of her writing and speeches, *Dear President Bush* (2006); and *Peace Mom: A Mother's Journey through Heartache to Activism* (2006). She was awarded the U.S. Peace Memorial Foundation's Peace Prize in 2009.

Although still best known for her opposition to the Iraq war, Sheehan has continued her activism, protesting the war policies of later administrations, running for office, and becoming active in the Peace and Freedom Party.

George,... your reckless and wanton foreign policies killed my son, Spc. Casey Austin Sheehan, in the illegal and unjust war on Iraq.. Helping to bring about your political downfall will be the most noble accomplishment of my life, and it will bring justice for my son and the hundreds of other brave Americans and tens of thousands of innocent Iraqis your lies have killed.

Cindy Sheehan

Robert Shetterly 2005

Samantha Smith

Student, peace activist; b. 1972, d.1985

. . . if we could be friends by just getting to know each other better, then what are our countries really arguing about? Nothing could be more important than not having a war if a war could kill everything.

From about 1950 to 1991, the United States and the Soviet Union were engaged in an antagonistic relationship, referred to as the Cold War. Neither side fired a shot (which would have meant a hot war), but both sides built more and more nuclear weapons, each escalating the number and size of the weapons in response to the perceived threat from the other. Hundreds of millions of people in both countries lived in fear that either by aggression or by accident a war would begin and everything would be annihilated—perhaps the whole world destroyed.

In 1982, Samantha Smith was a frightened ten-year-old girl living in the small community of Manchester, Maine. One day she asked her mother, Jane, if she would write to Yuri Andropov, the premier of the Soviet Union, and ask him whether the Soviet Union intended to start a war. Samantha's mother replied, "Why don't you?" Samantha did, and Premier Andropov wrote her back, inviting her to come to the Soviet Union to meet Russian people and see that they were peace-loving and had no desire to start a war.

Samantha's trip to the Soviet Union was a great success. She made lasting friendships with Russian children. She was so inspired that she became an international spokesperson for peace, traveling as far as Japan to talk with people about the necessity for stopping the Cold War and finding a way to live together. The stakes were too high not to find a way to peace.

Tragically, in 1985, Samantha and her father died in a plane crash as the plane attempted to land at Maine's Lewiston-Auburn Regional Airport. Smith, who, at age thirteen, had become something of a celebrity after her trip to the Soviet Union, was returning home after filming a television program. More than one thousand people attended her funeral, and Mikhail Gorbachev sent a personal message: "Everyone in the Soviet Union who has known Samantha Smith will forever remember the image of the American girl who, like millions of Soviet young men and women, dreamt about peace, and about friendship between the peoples of the United States and the Soviet Union."

Ronald Reagan also sent his condolences, writing, "Perhaps you can take some measure of comfort in the knowledge that millions of Americans, indeed millions of people, share the burdens of your grief. They also will cherish and remember Samantha, her smile, her idealism and unaffected sweetness of spirit."

A life-size bronze statue of Smanatha stands outside the State House in Augusta, Maine. The statue features her warm smile as she reaches out to release a dove of peace. Samantha made a huge difference in the way Russians and Americans thought about the Cold War, the humanity of one another, and the possibility of peace.

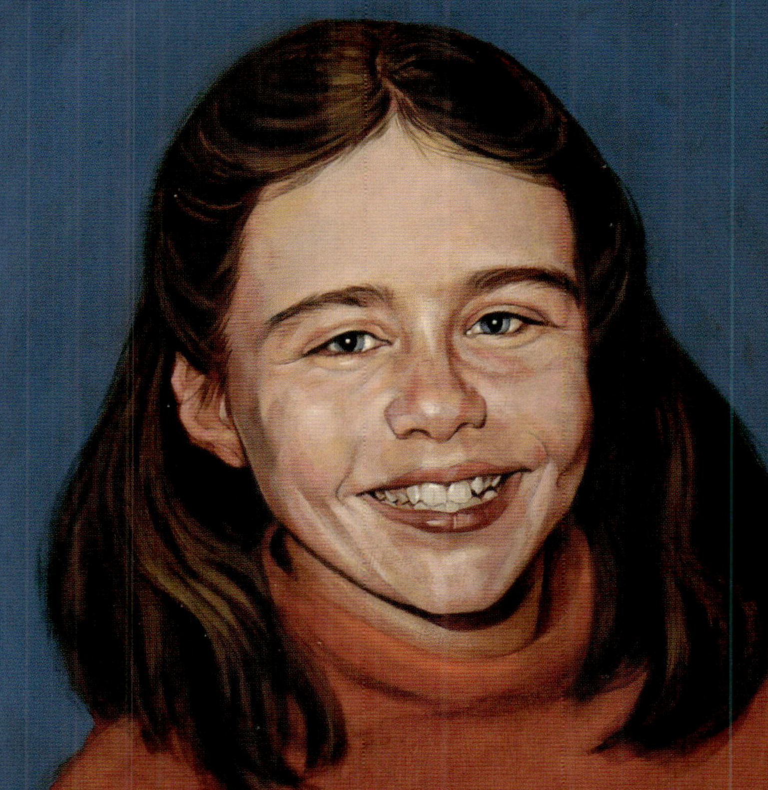

Samantha Smith
... if we could be friends by just getting to know each other better,
then what are our countries really arguing about? Nothing could be
more important than not having a war if a war could kill
everything.

David Swanson

Author, activist, agitator; b. 1969

It can be painful to realize that people you look up to as leaders recklessly waste human lives for no good reason. . . . The difficulty is not believing that they would tell enormous lies, but in believing that they would commit enormous crimes.

In 2011, when David Swanson learned that former Vice President Dick Cheney was planning a visit to Charlottesville, Virginia, he emailed a letter to local law enforcement asking them to arrest Cheney for conspiracy to commit torture. Shortly thereafter, Cheney canceled his visit. For this provocative act, Charlottesville's weekly independent newspaper, *The Hook,* named Swanson runner-up for Charlottesville's Person of the Year.

David Swanson is a radical journalist and activist for peace. Born December 1, 1969, in New York City, he has built his life and career around speaking out against torture and war and making the case against corrupt government practices. He was a fierce critic of the Bush administration's policies and continues to speak out against policies that promote violence and injustice. Swanson is cofounder and executive director of World BEYOND War, and has been active in many protest groups, including Veterans for Peace and the Green Shadow Cabinet. He is a leading figure in American alternative media, blogging on his personal website, davidswanson.org, and at warisacrime.org. He hosts *Talk World Radio* and is the campaign coordinator for RootsAction, an "online initiative dedicated to galvanizing Americans who are committed to economic fairness, equal rights, civil liberties, environmental protection—and defunding endless wars."

In the 1990s, Swanson earned a master's degree in philosophy at the University of Virginia, where he developed his "clarity and creativity of thought." Becoming "aware of how radically differently people have viewed the world in other times and places," Swanson began to work for radical change. As a student, he was active in the campaign for a living wage. After graduating, he worked briefly as a mainstream journalist, first at *The News Virginian* and later at *Culpeper News.* Frustrated by the censorship of mainstream editors, he sought out alternative media sources to publish his writing.

Swanson became directly involved in politics when he acted as the press secretary for Dennis Kucinich's 2004 presidential campaign. For five years, he was the director of communications for ACORN (Association of Community Organizations for Reform Now), a nonprofit group that advocated for social justice. Together, all these experiences have shaped and refined the worldview that permeates his writing and activism: "I came to appreciate the significance of dumping our money into a war machine rather than schools, houses, green energy, all the things we actually value. And I see the mass murder of people, which is what war is, as the most awful thing we allow to be done that could be easily prevented."

A prolific writer, Swanson has authored and contributed to roughly one book per year since 2008, when he wrote the introduction to Dennis Kucinich's book *The 35 Articles of Impeachment and the Case for Prosecuting George W. Bush.* His latest is *The Monroe Doctrine at 200 and What to Replace It With* (2023). Swanson's work has earned him several prestigious awards, including the U.S. Peace Memorial Foundation's Peace Prize in 2018. On a mission to change minds, Swanson writes, "I would like 'just war' to sound as offensive as 'charitable rape' or 'humanitarian slavery' or 'benevolent child abuse,' and I know that it can sound that offensive because it sounds so to me."

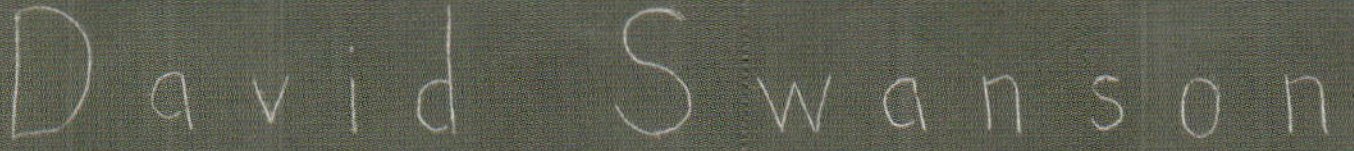
David Swanson

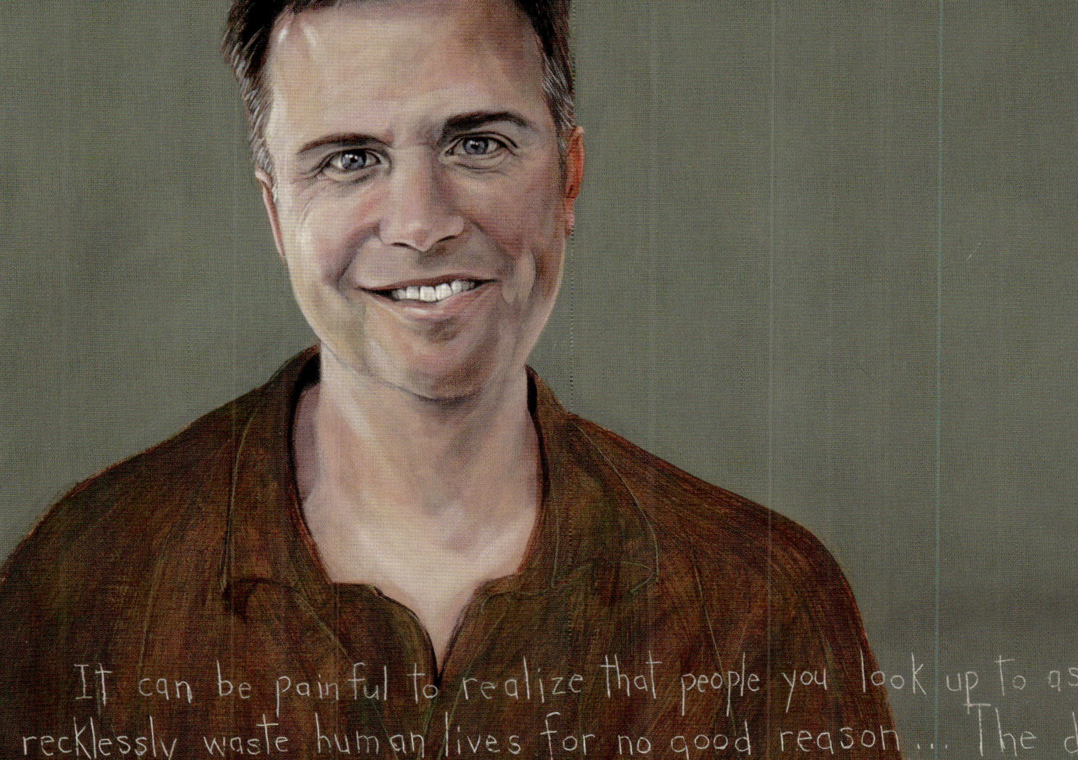
It can be painful to realize that people you look up to as leaders recklessly waste human lives for no good reason... The difficulty is not in believing that they would tell enormous lies, but in believing that they would commit enormous crimes.

V (Eve Ensler)

Playwright, performer, feminist; b. 1953

I am proposing that we reconceive the dream. That we consider what would happen if security were not the point of our existence. That we find freedom, aliveness, and power not from what contains, locates, or protects us but from what dissolves, reveals, and expands us.

V (formerly Eve Ensler) shattered taboos with her wildly successful play, *The Vagina Monologues,* which celebrates women's strength and sexuality. The play has been performed around the world and translated into more than forty-five languages. Its success inspired V to create V-Day, a global movement to stop violence against women and girls.

V suffered violence as a girl growing up in Scarsdale, New York. Behind the white picket fence facade of her upper-middle-class home, her alcoholic father abused her. She eventually escaped to college but became addicted to alcohol and drugs. At age twenty-three, she married the boyfriend who helped her get clean and adopted his teenaged son. Although she soon began writing plays, her work didn't receive wide acclaim until she wrote *The Vagina Monologues* in 1996. She interviewed more than two hundred women for the play, which was first performed in the basement of a Greenwich Village café. It won an Obie Award in 1997 for best new play.

Many women approached V after her performances to talk about their own experiences, particularly as victims of violence. Their stories led her to the creation of V-Day. Since its founding in 1998, V-Day has educated millions about violence against women and girls and raised more than seventy million dollars for antiviolence organizations around the world through local benefit performances of *The Vagina Monologues* and other provocative events. V-Day has helped support more than eleven thousand antiviolence programs in local communities and safe houses from the Democratic Republic of the Congo to Haiti, Kenya, South Dakota, Egypt, and Iraq.

Through her work with V-Day, V has visited more than forty countries. She has interviewed women in devastated communities who have been raped and tortured, lost their families to war, and suffered other forms of violence. Their stories, as well as her own, informed V's book *Insecure at Last: Losing It in a Security-Obsessed World* (2006), which examined how the current obsession with security undermines our humanity. "Real security cannot be bought or arranged or accomplished with bombs. It is deeper. It is a process. It is the acute awareness that we are all utterly interdependent and that one action by one being in one town has consequences everywhere. Real security is the ability to tolerate mystery, complexity, ambiguity—indeed hungering for these things."

In 2009, V testified before the Senate Committee on Foreign Relations on "Confronting Rape and Other Forms of Violence Against Women in Conflict Zones." The hearing focused on the Democratic Republic of the Congo (DRC), which the United Nations has called the rape capital of the world. The next year, V and V-Day opened the City of Joy in the DRC, a haven for women who have survived violence, providing housing, education, therapy, creative arts, and other resources to help women heal and empower them to become leaders in their country.

A self-described nomad and creative who lives alone, V continues to write plays, films, books, and magazine articles. *Reckoning*, V's 2023 memoir covering forty years of performance and activism, was touted by Naomi Klein as an "eclectic call to heal our broken world."

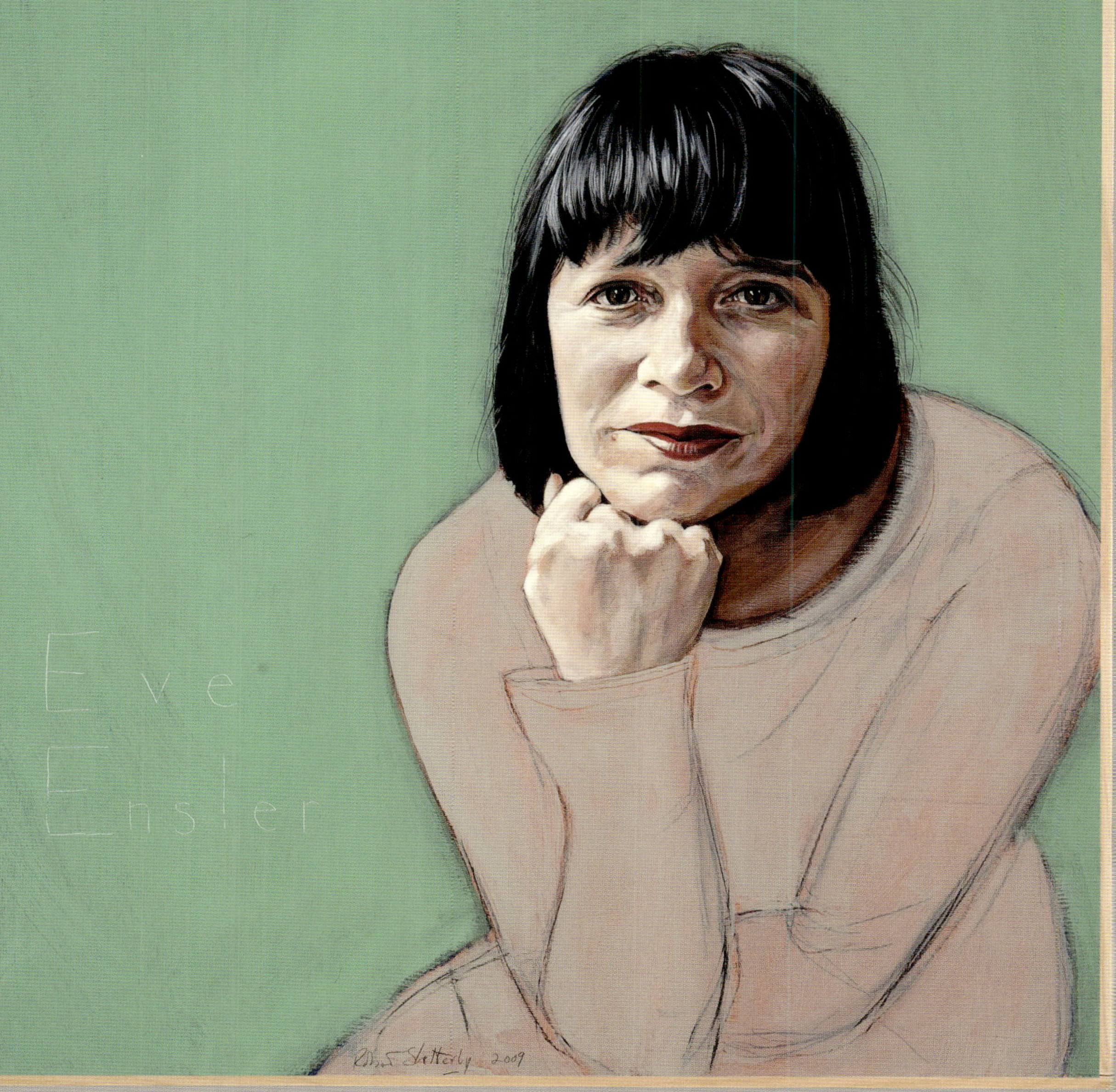
I am proposing that we reconceive the dream. That we consider what would happen if security were not the point of our existence. That we find freedom, aliveness, and power not from what contains, locates, or protects us but from what dissolves, reveals, and expands us.
Eve Ensler

Alice Walker

Novelist, essayist, poet, activist; b. 1944

The male leaders / of Earth / appear to have abandoned / their very senses / . . . They murder humans and other / animals / forests and rivers and mountains / every day / they are in office / and never seem to notice it. / They eat and drink devastation.

Women of the world, / Women of the world, / Is this devastation Us?

Alice Walker is a world-famous writer and activist, best known for her work in the civil rights and feminist movements. She was born on February 9, 1944, in Eatonton, Georgia, the youngest in a family of eight children. Her father worked as a sharecropper and her mother as a maid. To keep her daughter safe and away from field work,, Alice's mother enrolled her in first grade at the age of four. Throughout her childhood, Alice excelled academically while attending segregated schools.

At age eight, Walker was shot accidentally in her right eye with a BB gun while playing with her brothers. When scar tissue grew over the blind eye, she grew self-conscious about her appearance and withdrew to a solitary world of books and writing. Six years later, the scar tissue was removed, and she recovered her confidence. She went on to become a popular high school valedictorian. However, the years spent in isolation made a permanent impact on Walker's worldview. She learned to feel "empathy and a sense of kinship with other people she perceived to be afflicted." She also developed the powers of observation that serve her as a writer.

Walker earned a scholarship to Spelman College in Atlanta. On her first trip to Atlanta, she was ordered to move to the back of a bus, an incident that made her realize that she "would have to be politically active in order to achieve enough freedom to write at all." Later, Walker transferred to Sarah Lawrence College in Bronxville, New York, and graduated in 1965, at the height of the civil rights movement. In 1967, her first short story was published in the anthology *The Best Short Stories by Negro Writers*, edited by Langston Hughes.

In March 1967, Walker married Melvyn Leventhal, a Jewish civil rights lawyer. They moved to Mississippi, where their interracial marriage was illegal. The young couple were threatened and harassed. They had a daughter, Rebecca, in 1969; their marriage lasted seven more years. During this period, Walker built a name for herself as a writer—publishing poetry, fiction, and magazine journalism.

The peak of Walker's writing success came in 1982, when her novel *The Color Purple* was published. It won both the Pulitzer Prize and the National Book Award, became a bestseller, and was later made into an award-winning film by Stephen Spielberg. In total, Walker has published more than forty books, including fiction, poetry, criticism, and memoir.

Walker has protested the South African apartheid, the Iraq War, the Israeli occupation of Palestine, and female genital mutilation. In 2012, Walker declined to have *The Color Purple* published in Israel in protest of Israel's treatment of Palestinians, and she joined the nonviolent BDS (Boycott, Divestment, Sanctions) protest in hopes of inspiring change in Israel.

"I am tormented knowing what is being done to the children of Gaza . . . The Jewish child is precious, so is the Arab child. So is the African child and the Indian child and so on. To turn away from them is impossible for me."

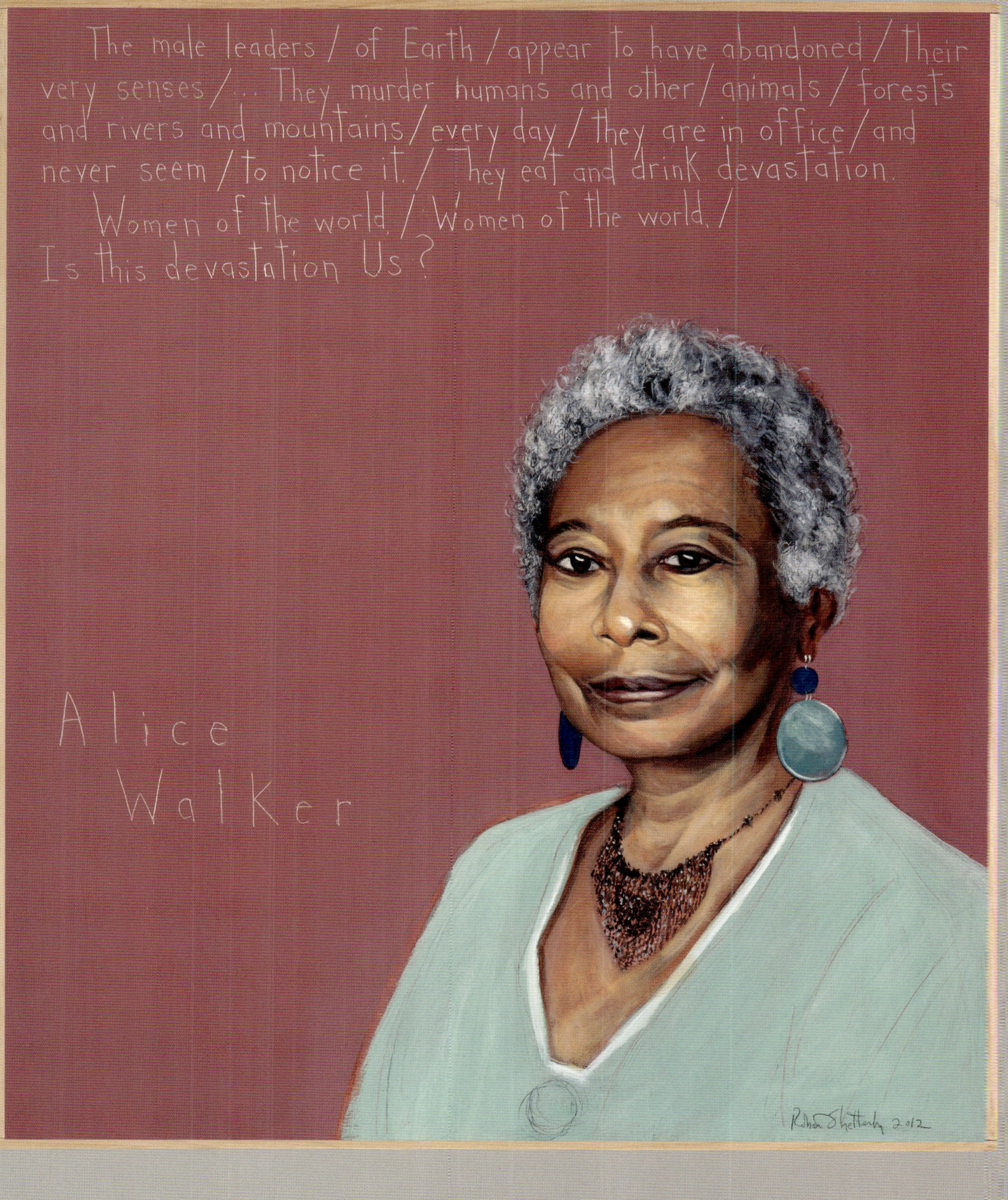

The male leaders / of Earth / appear to have abandoned / their
very senses / ... They murder humans and other / animals / forests
and rivers and mountains / every day / they are in office / and
never seem / to notice it. / They eat and drink devastation.
Women of the world, / Women of the world, /
Is this devastation Us?

Alice
Walker

Henry A. Wallace

U.S. vice president, peacemaker, progressive thinker, public servant; b. 1888, d.1965

Democracy . . . must apply itself to meeting the material need of men for work, for income, for goods, for health, for security, and to meeting their spiritual need for dignity, for knowledge, for self-expression, for adventure and for reverence. And it must succeed. The danger that it will be overthrown in favor of some other system is in direct proportion to its failure to meet those needs. . . . In the long run, democracy or any other political system will be measured by its deeds, not its words.

Henry A. Wallace was committed to progressive democracy in the United States and international cooperation toward peace and human rights. Near the end of World War II, he wrote, "When the time of peace comes, the citizen will again have a duty . . . the supreme duty of sacrificing the lesser interest for the greater interest of the general welfare. Those who write the peace must think of the whole world. There can be no privileged peoples."

Wallace was born in Adair County, Iowa, in 1888. His father, Henry Cantwell Wallace, was the secretary of agriculture under Warren G. Harding and Calvin Coolidge. Wallace's grandfather, Henry Wallace, edited and published agricultural periodicals. Wallace's love of plants and interest in plant breeding and corn was nurtured by his mentor, botanist George Washington Carver, who lived with the family while Carver was a graduate student in botany. After marrying Ilo Browne in 1914, Wallace bought a farm near Johnston, Iowa, where he continued to develop hybrid corn varieties. In 1926, he founded the successful Hi-Bred Corn Company, while revolutionizing the yield per acre for farmers.

Though his family had traditionally been Republican, seeing the harm inflicted on American farmers by the laissez-faire policies of Republican administrations, Wallace turned his support to the Democratic Party. When Franklin Delano Roosevelt was elected president in 1932, he appointed Wallace to serve as secretary of agriculture. Wallace designed sweeping New Deal farm legislation.

In 1940, Roosevelt yielded to entreaties to run for a third term but said he would do so only with Wallace as his running mate. Although the party bosses balked, Eleanor Roosevelt won them over at the convention with her speech: They must give the president what he wants, she said, because, with Hitler on the march and war looming, "this is no ordinary time."

The ticket won in a landslide. As the United States entered World War II, Wallace became a key member of the president's war cabinet and oversaw the Board of Economic Warfare. He quickly became a world leader, whose motto was "Peace, Prosperity, and Equality" and famously articulated the "common man" philosophy of the New Deal Democratic Party. Wallace was opposed to both economic and military imperialism and strongly in favor of what would become détente with the Soviet Union and international cooperation through the United Nations.

In 1944, the party bosses replaced Wallace with Harry Truman on the Democratic ticket. FDR said to Wallace, "You know, Henry, the things you believe in are all going to come someday. Your problem is that you're just too far ahead of your time." Under the Roosevelt/Truman administration Wallace served as secretary of commerce.

After Roosevelt's death, Wallace became editor of the progressive magazine *The New Republic,* and in 1948 ran for president under the newly established Progressive Party. His platform called for national health insurance, racial and gender equality, control of monopolies, and peaceful coexistence with the Soviet Union.

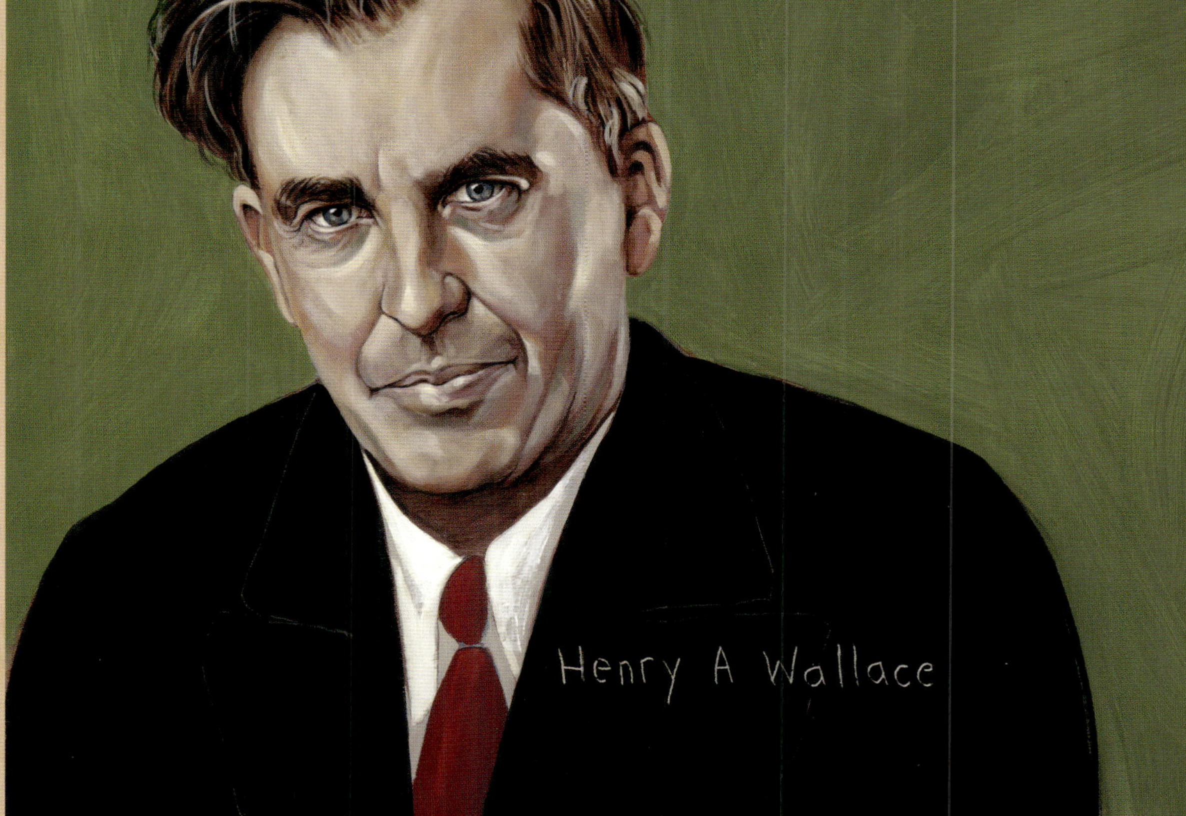

Democracy.. must apply itself to meeting the material need of men for work, for income, for goods, for health, for security, and to meeting the spiritual need for dignity, for knowledge, for self-expression, for adventure and for reverence. And it must succeed. The danger that it will be overthrown in favor of some other system is in direct proportion to its failure to meet those needs.. in the long run democracy or any other political system will be measured by its deeds, not its words.
Henry A Wallace

Shannon Watts

Antigun violence activist, organizer; b. 1971

Most mothers cannot fathom that their kids—even preschoolers and kindergarteners—will regularly spend part of their school day rehearsing for the possibility that someone with a gun will come into their school and murder as many people as possible.

How could lawmakers not act after twenty first graders and six educators had been slaughtered in the sanctity of an elementary school?

On May 24, 2022, tragedy struck our nation when an eighteen-year-old gunman, armed with a semiautomatic AR-15 rifle, entered Robb Elementary School in Uvalde, Texas, and murdered nineteen children and two educators. The attack, which marked at least the thirtieth shooting at a K-12 school that year, was devastating and all too familiar. Columbine High School. Sandy Hook Elementary School. Emanuel African Methodist Episcopal Church. Mandalay Bay. Pulse Nightclub. Marjory Stoneman Douglas High School. Innocent lives lost to random violence.

Ten years prior, a similar tragedy sparked Shannon Watts to found Moms Demand Action. December 14, 2012, started like any day. Watts dropped her children at school and began her work as a full-time mom—cleaning, cooking, shopping. She was folding laundry, watching the news, when a breaking story interrupted. Twenty children and six educators had been gunned down in their classrooms at Sandy Hook Elementary School in Newtown, Connecticut. She thought of her five children, sitting at their school desks at that very moment. Her heart ached for the loss of life and the suffering of these families. If thoughts and prayers alone were enough to prevent gun violence, she thought, Americans wouldn't get shot in our places of worship. She thought of her role models as a child—activists like Harriet Tubman and Susan B. Anthony, whose homes she had visited on school field trips while growing up in Rochester, New York. Turning to the teachings of her Buddhist faith, she sought to convert righteous anger into transformational change.

Watts used skills she had developed as a journalist with the University of Missouri's student newspaper, *The Maneater,* and as a communications executive in the Fortune 100 world to begin a conversation on Facebook. "This site is dedicated to action on gun control—not just dialogue about anti-gun violence," she posted. Watts urged women to march on Washington, D.C., to demand that legislators protect their children. Thousands rallied. Within months, she and hundreds of volunteers from around the country were lobbying the halls of Congress. A movement had started. Moms Demand Action soon became the largest gun-control lobby in the United States, with chapters in every state and the District of Columbia, working to elect gun-sense champions, educate gun owners on the importance of secure firearm storage, and push for better policies. Watts's book *Fight Like a Mother: How a Grassroots Movement Took on the Gun Lobby and Why Women Will Change the World* (2019) tells the story of her organizing efforts.

The killings in Uvalde highlight the seeming intractability of gun violence. Indeed, deaths by firearms in the United States continue to rise. Watts responds by saying, "Activism is like drips on a rock . . . [b]ut if you don't show up . . . then change never happens."

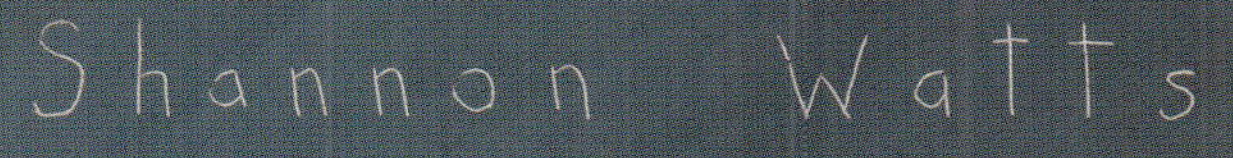

Shannon Watts

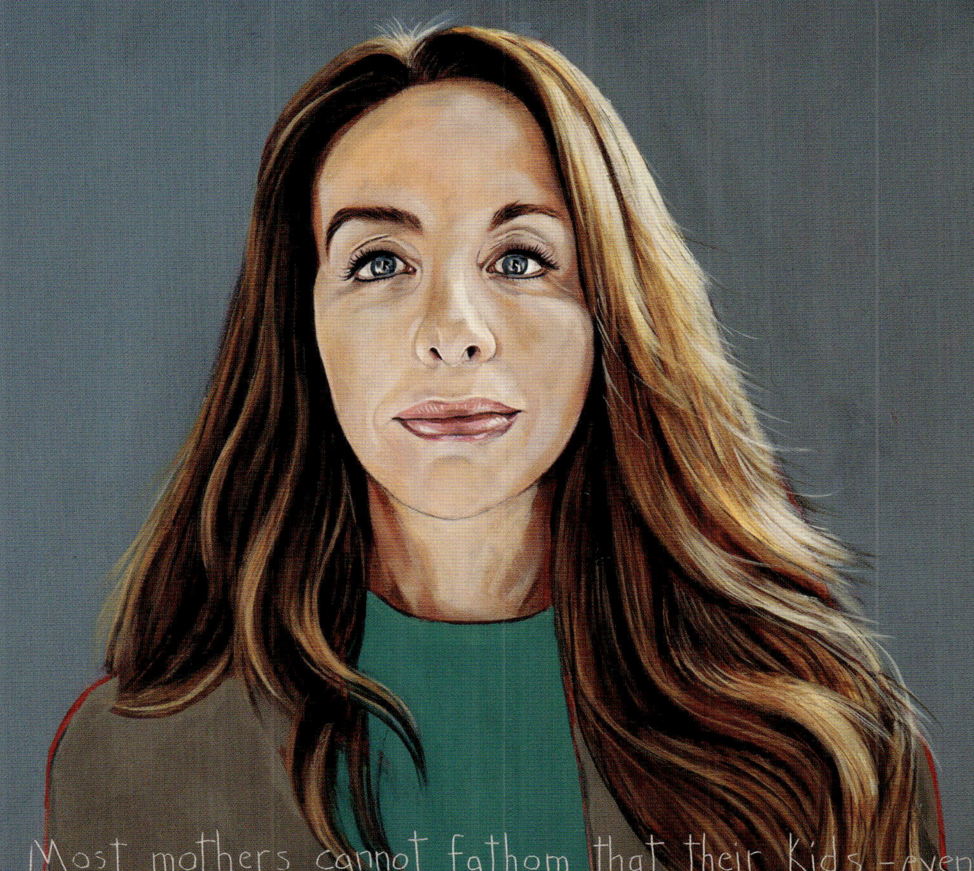

Most mothers cannot fathom that their kids — even preschoolers & kindergarteners — will regularly spend part of their school day rehearsing for the possibility that someone with a gun will come into their school and murder as many people as possible.
How could lawmakers not act after twenty first-graders and six educators had been slaughtered in the sanctity of an elementary school?

Craig Williams

Environmentalist, advocate for safe destruction of chemical weapons; b. 1948

With a six billion dollar budget against our four or five hundred dollar expense account, we realize you, the Pentagon, can hire more lawyers, get more studies, and pay more experts. But what you can't get is thousands of Kentuckians to support your plan. That is the one thing that we've got that you can't get. The people's will will prevail and we will stop this incinerator.

When Craig Williams and his wife, Teri, went to a community information meeting at the Blue Grass Army Depot nearly forty years ago, they were appalled to hear the army's plans to incinerate a huge arsenal of toxic chemical weapons dating back to World War I at several sites, including one just a few miles from their home in Madison County, Kentucky. Craig tells the story: "Teri looked at me and said, 'Somebody's got to do something about this.' And so, since I always do what my wife tells me, forty years later, here I am."

Williams began working with other citizen groups living near incinerator sites in the United States as well as sites in the Pacific and in Russia. They secured funding to hire experts to testify about the dangers of incineration and procured "documents that showed fourteen live agent releases from the stacks of . . . incinerators in the Pacific and in the Utah desert."

In response to citizen concerns, Congress directed the army to develop a program to study alternative technologies and developed the Assembled Chemical Weapons Assessment program, which identified "six technologies capable of closed-loop chemical destruction," where chemical weapons are neutralized without being released into the environment. Two of those were ultimately chosen to safely destroy the weapons.

Asked about his leadership in advocating for these changes, Williams stresses the importance of credibility. "Military and politicians can be caught lying on a Tuesday, be discovered misrepresenting the truth on Wednesday, then say something on that topic on Thursday and be believed," but the activist community does not have this luxury.

Grassroots organizations have worked collaboratively for almost four decades to bring about an "environmentally secure conclusion to the chemical weapons issue." The inaugural National Citizens Conference on Chemical Weapons was held in Richmond, Kentucky, in 1990. The movement continued to grow in stages, culminating in the formation of the Chemical Weapons Working Group, an international coalition focused on safe disposal.

Closer to home, Craig founded the Kentucky Environmental Foundation (KEF) and served as its executive director. He is also a charter member and chair of the Kentucky governor's Chemical Material Demilitarization Citizens' Advisory Commission and currently serves as cochair of the Kentucky Chemical Destruction Community Advisory Board.

NERVE is the prize-winning hour-long film about "the remarkable story of a small band of ordinary people who took on the world's most powerful bureaucracy—building an international movement from the ground up, transforming the way nations destroy their chemical weapons."

On July 7, 2023, the last remaining chemical weapons stored at the Blue Grass Army Depot in Richmond, Kentucky, were safely destroyed. At a community celebration of this momentous event, Williams honored his wife, Teri, thanking her for her care of the family, which made his work possible, adding, "And she is beautiful."

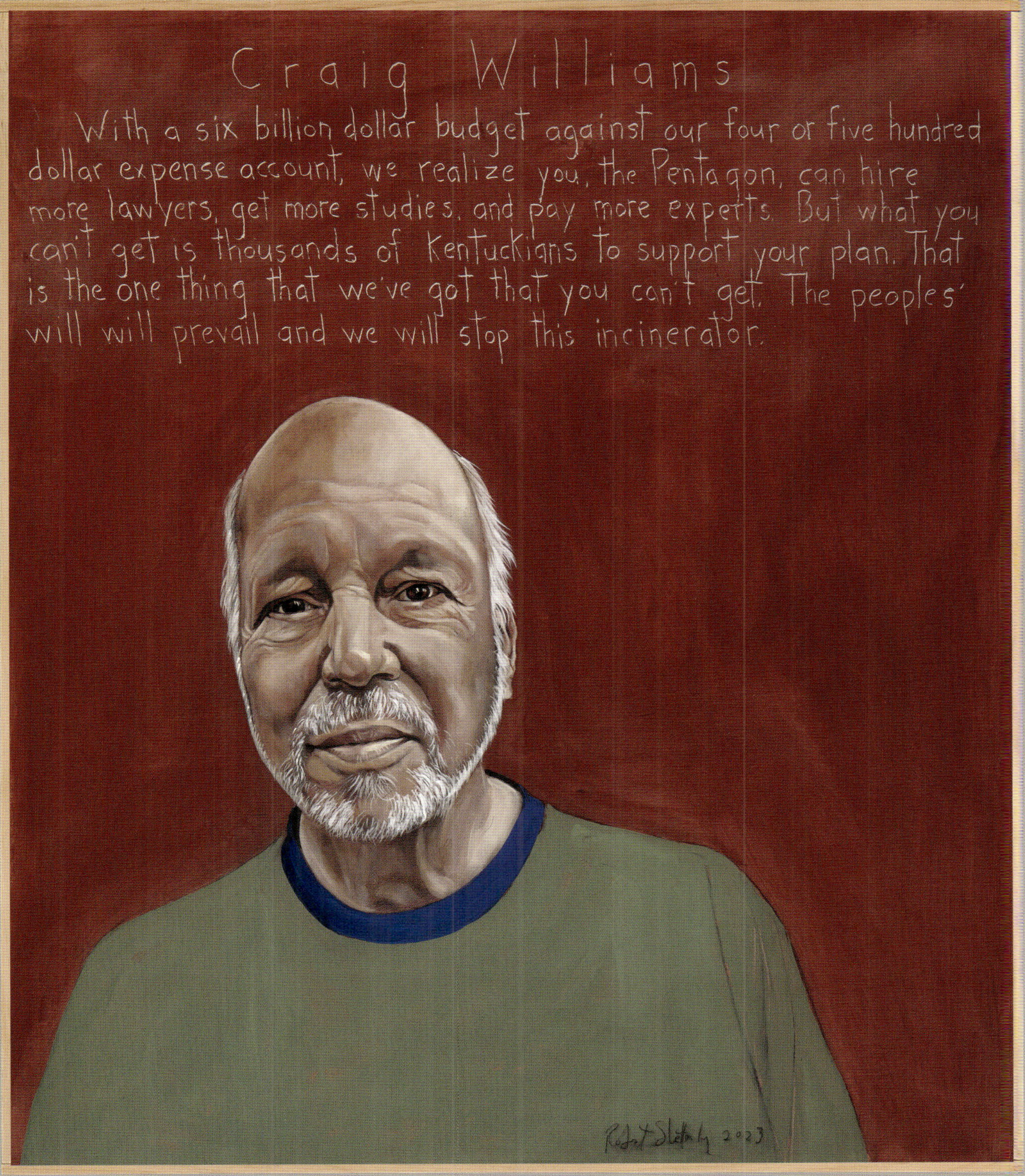

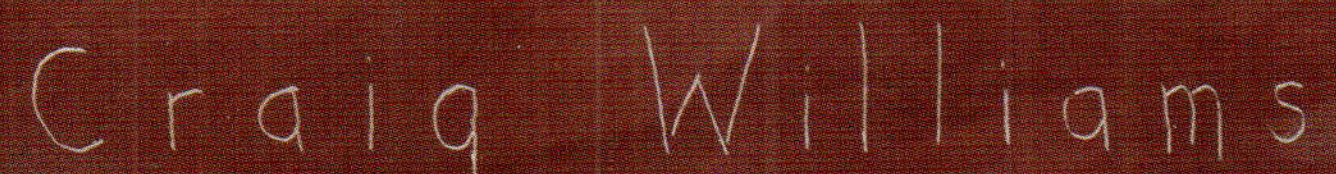

Craig Williams

With a six billion dollar budget against our four or five hundred dollar expense account, we realize you, the Pentagon, can hire more lawyers, get more studies, and pay more experts. But what you can't get is thousands of Kentuckians to support your plan. That is the one thing that we've got that you can't get. The peoples' will will prevail and we will stop this incinerator.

Jody Williams

Activist, writer, teacher, Nobel laureate; b. 1950

Militarists say that to gain peace we must prepare for war. I think we get what we prepare for. If we want a world where peace is valued, we must teach ourselves to believe that peace is not a "utopian vision" but a real responsibility that must be worked for each and every day in small and large ways. Any one of us can contribute to building a world where peace and justice prevail.

In 1992, Jody Williams cofounded and coordinated the International Campaign to Ban Landmines (ICBL). Originally backed by six nongovernmental organizations (NGOs), the campaign grew to represent more than thirteen hundred NGOs in over eighty-five countries. During the first five years, Williams was the ICBL's chief organizer, strategist, and spokesperson, coordinating with other governments, the United Nations, and the International Committee of the Red Cross. In 1997, the campaign achieved its goal: an international treaty banning antipersonnel land mines. Jody Williams was awarded the Nobel Peace Prize—the third American woman to receive this honor.

Addressing the Mine Ban Treaty–signing conference in Ottawa, Canada, Williams said, "It wasn't until the voice of civil society was raised to such a high degree that governments began to listen, that change began to move the world, with lightning and unexpected speed."

Williams trained to be a "voice of civil society" both in formal studies and as an activist working to build public awareness about U.S. policy in Central America. She graduated from the University of Vermont and received a master's degree in teaching Spanish and English as a second language (ESL) from the School for International Training in Brattleboro, Vermont. She earned a second master's degree in international relations at Johns Hopkins School of Advanced International Studies. For six years she worked on humanitarian relief projects for El Salvador. She coordinated the Nicaragua-Honduras Education Project, which involved leading fact-finding delegations in the region. She has also taught ESL in Mexico, the United Kingdom, and Washington, D.C.

Since her receipt of the Nobel for her work with ICBL, Williams has continued her mission of creating a more peaceful world. She works with other Nobel laureates for the organization PeaceJam "to inspire a new generation of peacemakers who will transform their local communities, themselves, and the world."

Since 2006, Williams has worked with the Nobel Women's Initiative, harnessing the laureates' influence "to promote the work of women working for peace, justice and equality." In 2019, in support of the Every Woman Coalition, she called for a treaty to end violence against women, and in 2020, she called upon Chevron to pay cleanup costs to the residents of the Lago Agrio oil field in Ecuador. She also continues to be a "campaign ambassador" for the ICBL.

Williams is the Sam and Cele Keeper Endowed Professor in Peace and Social Justice in the Graduate College of Social Work at the University of Houston, where she began teaching in 2003. She has received fifteen honorary degrees and other public recognitions and is the author of many essays and book contributions. She released her memoir in 2013: *My Name Is Jody Williams: A Vermont Girl's Winding Path to the Nobel Peace Prize.*

Described as a lifelong advocate of freedom, self-determination, and human and civil rights, Williams is quick to remind us that "[w]e must teach ourselves to believe that peace is not a 'utopian vision' but a responsibility that must be worked for each and every day."

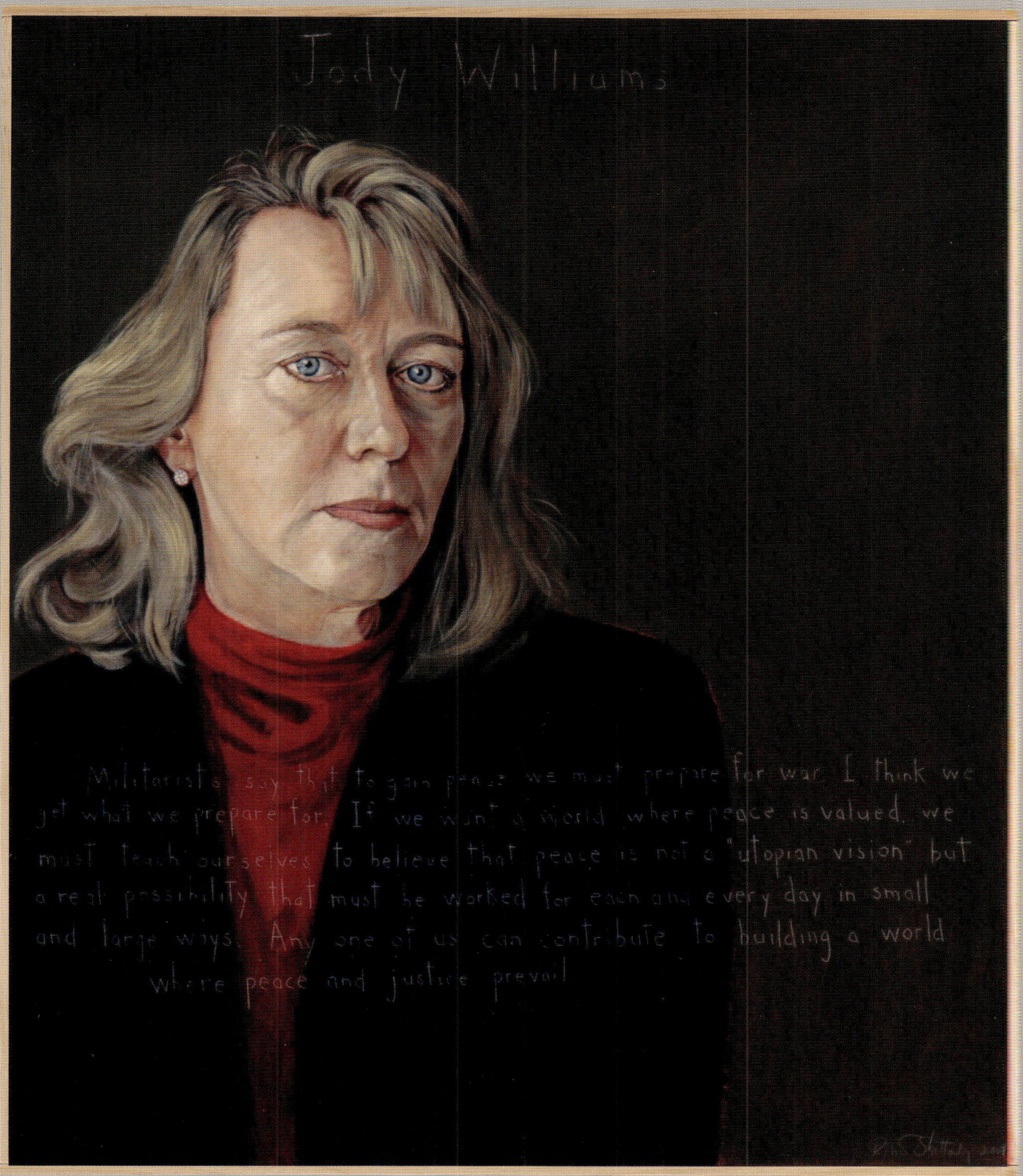

Jody Williams
Militarists say that to gain peace we must prepare for war. I think we get what we prepare for. If we want a world where peace is valued, we must teach ourselves to believe that peace is not a "utopian vision" but a real possibility that must be worked for each and every day in small and large ways. Any one of us can contribute to building a world where peace and justice prevail.

Ann Wright

Army colonel, foreign diplomat; b. 1946

*I have served my country for almost thirty years in some of the most isolated and dangerous parts
of the world. I want to continue to serve America. However, I do not believe in the policies of this
Administration and cannot—morally or professionally—defend or implement them. It is with heavy heart
that I must end my service to America and therefore resign. . . .*

Patriotism can manifest in many forms and has for Mary Ann Wright—as a career military woman, a State Department diplomat, and an influential spokesperson in the antiwar movement.

Wright grew up in Bentonville, Arkansas, and attended the University of Arkansas, where she earned a master's and a law degree. She also has a master's degree in national security affairs from the U.S. Naval War College. In her junior year at the University of Arkansas, after meeting with a visiting army recruiter, she attended a three-week army training program. That experience helped inform her decision to join the military.

For thirteen years, Wright was an active-duty soldier. She spent another sixteen years in the U.S. Army Reserves, retiring as a colonel. Part of her army work was special operations in civil affairs. In the event of invasions into other countries, Wright helped to develop "plans about how you interact with the civilian population, how you protect the facilities—sewage, water, electrical grids, libraries. . . . It's our obligation under the law of land warfare." After Wright was released from active duty, she joined the State Department. For the next sixteen years, she served as a foreign diplomat in many countries, including Nicaragua, Somalia, Uzbekistan, and Sierra Leone. She was on the team that reopened the U.S. embassy in Kabul, Afghanistan, in December 2001, after the fall of the Taliban to U.S. forces.

In all those years, Wright was proud to represent the United States. However, on March 13, 2003, the eve of the U.S. invasion of Iraq, Col. Ann Wright sent a letter of resignation to then Secretary of State Colin Powell. She felt that without the authorization of the U.N. Security Council, the U.S. invasion and occupation of an oil-rich Arab Muslim country would be a disaster. Only two other State Department officials resigned at that time in protest of the imminent invasion. In an interview, Wright explained that, in the Foreign Service, "[y]our job is to implement the policies of an administration. . . . If you strongly disagree with any administration's policies, and wish to speak out, your only option is to resign. I understood that and that's one of the reasons I resigned—to give myself the freedom to talk out."

Talk out she has. Her sense of patriotism called her to become an antiwar activist. She worked with Cindy Sheehan organizing Camp Casey and appeared in the documentary *Uncovered: The Truth About the Iraq War*. She travels and lectures on foreign policy issues. She has been arrested many times for protesting military policies and has referred to herself cheerfully as a "felon for peace." Her antiwar efforts have included work with the Gaza Freedom March and opposition to Israel's 2023 invasion of Gaza. In 2017, Wright received the U.S. Peace Prize from the U.S. Peace Memorial Foundation "for courageous antiwar activism, inspirational peace leadership, and selfless citizen diplomacy."

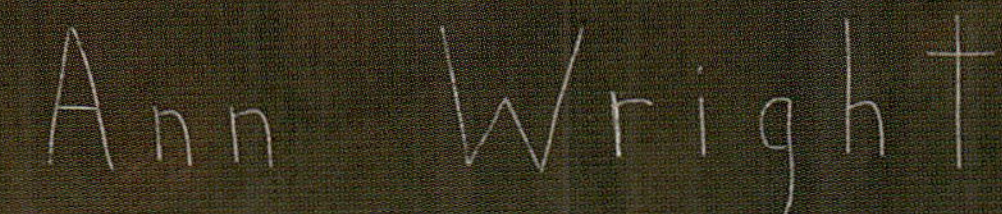
Ann Wright

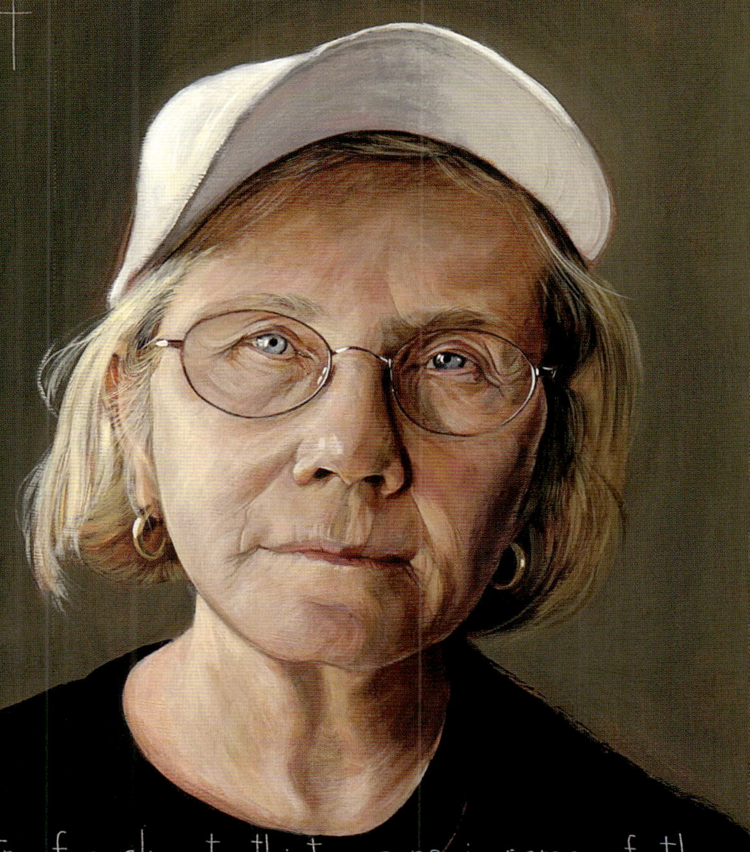
I have served my country for almost thirty years in some of the
most isolated and dangerous parts of the world. I want to
continue to serve America. However, I do not believe in the policies
of this Administration and cannot — morally or professionally —
defend or implement them. It is with heavy heart that I must
end my service to America and therefore resign...

Howard Zinn

Historian, political theorist, educator; b. 1922, d. 2010

The rule of law does not do away with the unequal distribution of wealth and power,
but reinforces that inequality with the authority of law. It allocates wealth and poverty
in such complicated and indirect ways as to leave the victim bewildered.

oward Zinn was born into a working-class family in Brooklyn, New York, and, though he had few formal educational opportunities, he developed a strong social consciousness while working as a shipfitter and avidly reading the novels of Charles Dickens. Flying bombing missions in World War II shaped his opposition to war. After military service he earned a doctorate in history at Columbia University and then taught at Spelman College in Georgia, a school for Black women, where he was active in the civil rights movement. In 1964, he moved to Boston University and became a prominent, outspoken critic of the Vietnam War.

Zinn is best known for his history of America through the perspective of "those outside of the political and economic establishment," *A People's History of the United States* (1980). Up until his death in 2010, Zinn remained an active advocate for the underclass, a proponent of world peace, and an articulate critic of corporate power and greed supported by governmental collusion.

"We need new ways of thinking," said Zinn. "We need to rethink our position in the world. We need to stop sending weapons to countries that oppress other people or their own people. We need to be resolute in our decision that we will not go to war, whatever reason is conjured up by the politicians or the media, because war in our time is always indiscriminate, a war against innocents, a war against children. War is terrorism, magnified a hundred times.

". . . We cannot be secure by limiting our liberties, as some of our political leaders are demanding, but only by expanding them. . . .

"We should take our example not from the military and political leaders shouting 'retaliate' and 'war' but from the doctors and nurses and . . . firemen and policemen who have been saving lives in the midst of mayhem, whose first thoughts are not vengeance but compassion, not violence but healing."

The rule of law does not do away with the unequal distribution of wealth and power, but reinforces that inequality with the authority of law. It allocates wealth and poverty ... in such complicated and indirect ways as to leave the victim bewildered.

Howard Zinn

Acknowledgments

The *Americans Who Tell the Truth* portrait project began as a solitary endeavor, an act of art therapy for myself to help me reconcile with the violent hypocrisies of this country's difficult history. The success of AWTT, however, has been due to the many people who have contributed in so many ways to its expansion and educational mission, people who have helped to shape it into a project far greater than I could have imagined.

For many years now a core team has made the decisions about the implementation of our mission and the formulation of our educational work—my son, Aran Shetterly, executive director; Connie Carter, our education director; and Kristie Gonzalez, our director of strategic engagement. Aran, Connie, and Kristie have been totally dedicated to this project. They combine creativity, wisdom, and good humor with practicality. My gratitude is immense. As much as the portrait subjects, they have been my teachers.

AWTT began and is still, at its core, an art project. Our belief in the power of art to focus attention, to inspire, to enrich and teach is based in great part on the quality of art. I often say that good art authenticates its own message. If people recognize the quality of the work, they are likely to give credence to its message. Each portrait carries an ethical, political, and historical message, but prior to the message I attempt to make a good painting and honor the person with as good a likeness as I can manage. The extent to which I am successful is due in large part to the critical advice of my partner, Gail Page, also an artist, whose advice I seek at various stages of every portrait. I could not possibly exaggerate my gratitude for her willingness to tell me the truth when I am struggling with a likeness, even when I may not be keen to hear it.

Americans Who Tell the Truth has now a very actively engaged and dedicated board of directors. Marion Morris, Sherry Streeter, Jamie Kilbreth, Eric Sass, and John Diamond advise on every important decision we make and help with the funding to keep the education work going.

Central to our mission is matching an inspiring narrative with each portrait. Over the years we've had a great team of researchers/writers. These include Anne Cushman, Rachel Mack, Jeffrey Harris, Julie Gronlund, Ashley Kang, Richard Sassaman, Adrienne Chamberlin, Daegan Miller, Laura Rothstein, Lynn Gonzalez, and Pamela Slowkowski. And in preparation for each book the bios have to be edited to half their length by Kathleen Caldwell, who also does a lot of the management of the AWTT website. Kathleen edits my blog writing, too.

I want to thank a few of the strong advocates for AWTT who have arranged exhibits and worked hard to increase our impact: Jim Clark, Kate Laissle, Gladys McCormick, Julia Ganson, Rose Viviano, Michele Hemenway, Laura Rothstein, Joe Gutmann, Nancy Doda, Argy Nestor, and Ingrid Sellers. Jim Clark has promoted the inclusion of AWTT in the curriculum of Syracuse University for more than eight years and arranged the only, to this point, exhibit of the entire collection at the university in 2018. Michele Hemenway, from Louisville, was the first teacher to begin building an AWTT curriculum for her classroom in 2004 and has worked with us ever since. And Chris Wood of BALE (Building a Local Living Economy) in South Royalton, VT, has mounted many AWTT shows.

I want to mention Ellie Richard from Asheville, NC, and Meryl Baier of Ipswich, MA, and a team of volunteers from Charlottesville, VA (Julie Gronlund Bruce Gordon, Linda Winecoff, Emma Terry, Jacqueline Langholtz, Lynne Levine, Catherine Spear, Michael Spear, Andrea Douglas, Enid Krieger). They pioneered novel ways of engaging entire communities in participation with AWTT exhibits.

These people as staff and board members have made invaluable contributions to the viability of

AWTT: Bob Sargent, Scott Gardiner, Rachel Freedman, Dud Hendrick, Betty Burkes, Charlie Clements.

I want to thank Fred Schall and John Hofstetter for their wonderful redesign and creative programming of our website, and to thank Ken Woisard for his excellent photography of the portraits.

Thank you to all the schools and other organizations that have hosted exhibitions and engaged with our curriculum. And thank you to all the people who have supported this project with donations and purchases of cards and posters, puzzles, mugs, and tote bags.

A big thank-you to the venues that have ongoing exhibits of some AWTT portraits: the PEG Center in Newburyport, Massachusetts, and Thomas College in Waterville, Maine.

Many of the portrait subjects have been suggested to me by people writing from around the world. I thank them all; they have alerted me to many important stories and have increased the range of the project.

A special thanks to Lynne Elizabeth, our editor at New Village Press, who believed in the project and made the series of AWTT books happen. She's been a delight to work with.

Lastly, I want to offer my immense gratitude to the portrait subjects themselves. This book is about peacemakers. Peace in this country and in many parts of the world is merely an interlude, a pause to rearm, to develop ever more efficient and devastating weapons, a time to stimulate fear and ideological hatred. Metaphorically those interludes are not unlike the Christmas Truce in World War I, when, for twenty-four hours on Christmas Day in 1914, German and English soldiers ceased slaughtering one another, and, in opposition to their officers, climbed out of the opposing trenches to celebrate their fraternity. Afterward the same men who had just been trading photographs of loved ones, lighting one another's cigarettes, and playing soccer went back to killing. Why? Why didn't they simply throw down their weapons and walk away from the idiocy of that war once they had seen one another as human beings? This book shows the portraits and tells the stories of people who, had they been there in World War I, would most likely have organized continuing resistance to officers and orders. These people have steadfast perseverance and courageous determination in trying to bend the arc of our history toward peace. They act out of love for victims and with rage at the warmakers.

Peacemaking, like war making, is a choice. Teaching the one instead of the other is a choice. Building an economy on war making rather than peacemaking is another choice. Allowing the architects and profiteers of war making, who manipulate with fear, to determine domestic and foreign policy is yet another choice. Let the courage and compassion of peacemakers be our guide to rethinking our choices, resisting violence with nonviolence, choosing diplomacy, and shaping the common good.